TWENTY
DECORATIVE
CARVING
PROJECTS
in Period Styles

TWENTY
DECORATIVE
CARVING
PROJECTS
in Period Styles

STEVE BISCO

GUILD OF MASTER CRAFTSMAN
PUBLICATIONS

First published 2010 by
Guild of Master Craftsman Publications Ltd
Castle Place, 166 High Street, Lewes,
East Sussex BN7 1XU

Text © Steve Bisco, 2010
Copyright in the Work © GMC Publications Ltd, 2010

ISBN 978-1-86108-694-5

A catalogue record for this book is available from the British Library.

PHOTOGRAPHIC CREDITS
All photographs taken by *Steve Bisco*, apart from the following:
Anthony Bailey, pp. 6–7, 16 (Celtic Cross, Linenfold Panel, Renaissance Panel),
17 (Chippendale Ribbon Festoon), 21, 34, 55, 73, 89, 115, 127, 137, 153, 163 and 189.
Josephine Bisco, pp. 2 and 179 (Photo 19), by kind permission of Mari Demauro

ASSOCIATE PUBLISHER *Jonathan Bailey*
PRODUCTION MANAGER *Jim Bulley*
MANAGING EDITOR *Gerrie Purcell*
PROJECT EDITOR *Gill Parris*
MANAGING ART EDITOR *Gilda Pacitti*
DESIGN *Terry Jeavons*

Set in Plantin
Colour origination by GMC Reprographics
Printed and bound in China by Hing Yip Printing Co. Ltd

CONTENTS

INTRODUCTION

I took up woodcarving many years ago out of necessity. Having spent my leisure time exploring the stately homes and historic buildings of England, I found it was necessary for me to have some period carved ornament in my own home and, not having sufficient funds to buy a stately home, it was clear I would have to make my own.

Being the son of a carpenter, I had grown up with the understanding that if you wanted something you just got some wood and made it. So, with a very poor set of tools and even poorer skills, I set about carving an oak mantelpiece with a 'briar rose' frieze on it. Despite these handicaps it worked out quite well, so I persevered. Slowly, year by year, I found the confidence to try more complex pieces and found that, with time and patience, you can indeed have some of the trappings of a stately home in a modest family house.

One of the things that made my progress slower (apart from being saddled with a 'day job') was a lack of suitable patterns to follow. Yes, there were plenty of books that would show you 'how to carve' – but very few had complete projects to follow. I hope this book will help to fill that gap and provide you with all the information you need to create your own 'home gallery' of period carvings.

The 20 projects are arranged roughly in order of difficulty, so if you are new to carving you could start at Project 1 (the Celtic Cross) and, over a few years, depending on the time you have available, work your way through to Project 20, a limewood foliage carving in the style of the great master Grinling Gibbons. By that time you will be an accomplished woodcarver. If you already have some experience, you will still find the simpler projects useful as many of them can be completed in a few days - very handy if your carving time is limited.

However you choose to use this book, I hope you will get as much pleasure from these projects as I did. Just a word of warning, though – your home will gradually fill up with woodcarvings, so you may need a bigger house!

ABOUT THIS BOOK

This book is for the hobby woodcarver, of any level of experience. It contains 20 decorative carving projects which you can make. Each one represents a particular period or style throughout the historical spectrum and is designed to capture the spirit of that period or style. Nine of these projects have been published in *Woodcarving* magazine, one in *Woodworking Plans & Projects*, and ten have been created specially for this book. The projects are intended for the 'home gallery' and can be displayed on walls and cabinets in your home. They will be of particular interest to anyone who likes to visit stately homes and historic buildings, and wants to create that feel at home.

Each project includes:
• A pattern you can copy to full size
• Step-by-step photos
• Instructions so you can follow the process

Projects range from quick and simple to long and complex, so you can develop your skills by trying more challenging pieces as you progress. At the end of each project you will have developed new skills, gained an understanding of another style, and created something you will be proud to display in your home.

CREATING YOUR 'HOME GALLERY'

If you are lucky enough to live in a large house you will have no shortage of space to display any number and size of woodcarvings. If, like myself and most other people, you live in a modest family home, your display space will be more limited. You may also be a little bashful about displaying carvings that seem too 'grand' for your modest home. The projects in this book are designed to fit into the average house (with the possible exception of Project 19 which is an exercise in large-scale carving). They have, in most cases, been scaled down from period originals or been specially designed to capture the spirit of a period in a compact piece.

As for being 'grand', I admit that some of them are. That is their beauty and an essential feature of their period style. Before the bleakness of modernism and minimalism came to dominate design in the twentieth century, people delighted in elaborate decoration and, without it, there would be no decorative woodcarving. I believe the human spirit needs more than plain surfaces and square edges, and it is natural to embellish surfaces with shapes and colours that lift our spirits and satisfy our creative instincts.

If you did not appreciate the decorative styles of our ancestors, I doubt you would be reading this book, so I will not preach to the converted. I will just urge you to overcome any shyness you may feel about embellishing your home with carvings that some non-carvers may consider to display 'delusions of grandeur'. Let them think what they will. You will have the pleasure of knowing that you can create things of beauty for your own home which, normally, only the wealthy would have had access to in their stately piles.

The 'project approach'

A friend once said to me when looking at one of my carvings, 'I wouldn't know where to start'. Knowing where to start is, of course, the first step towards completing any project. It is often the most difficult step in the whole process. Once you have been shown where to start, the rest often falls into place behind it. That is why this book follows the 'project approach' by setting out all the key steps you need to follow to turn a block of wood into a finished carving.

The step-by-step process is set out in pictures and instructions for each of the 20 projects. Each one is complete in itself so you don't need to keep referring back to other parts of the book to find out how to use a particular technique or create a particular finish.

While this does create some repetition in the book as a whole, it makes each project easier to follow. Some processes, like tracing and cutting round the pattern, are common to most projects, but as the projects progress the range of operations and techniques becomes ever greater. Every project is different, and as you work your way through the book your range of carving and finishing skills will inevitably expand by practical experience.

A picture is worth a thousand words, and anything you don't pick up from the text should be apparent to you in the photos. Read through the whole project first before you start, then follow the steps from 'where to start' through to the finish.

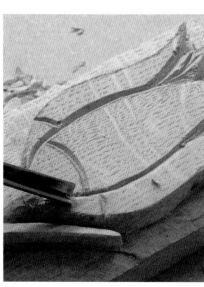

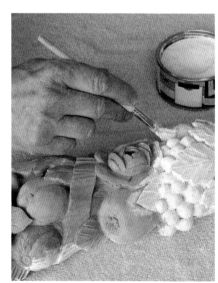

USING THE PATTERNS

Each of the projects has a pattern you can enlarge to create a full-size tracing. Each pattern is set out with gridlines which equate to 1in (25mm) squares when blown up to actual size. It is up to you what size you make your carving, but if you want to make it the same size as my original and relate it to the measurements quoted in the instructions, you should enlarge the drawing so the gridlines are 1in apart.

The easiest way to enlarge the pattern to full size is with an enlarging photocopier. Experiment until you get the pattern as near as possible to the 1in scale. You can also scan it into your computer.

Another way is to photograph the page with a digital camera and print it out in sections on your computer. If you use this method, don't put the camera too close to the page, as it will create a 'fish-eye lens' effect causing the sides of the drawing to bulge outwards. Place the camera further back, get it square on to the page, and use the zoom to focus in on the page. When you look at it on the computer, check there is no significant distortion in the gridlines – they should be straight, parallel and square.

You can also do it the old-fashioned way, which is more flexible and often easier. Just mark out a large sheet of paper with 1in gridlines – the same number as on the drawing. Mark reference letters and numbers in the squares along the top and sides of the book page and your sheet. Now just draw whatever lines you see in each square onto your sheet in the same square. Tidy up the lines at the end, and you will have a full-size drawing. Using this method, you can easily scale a drawing up or down to any size you want just by adjusting the width of your gridlines. This method is used in Project 19 to scale up a drawing to four times its original size.

When you have produced your full-size pattern, you must trace it onto the wood. You can place the paper directly on the wood, but it is better to trace it first onto tracing paper. This allows you to see the grain of the wood and adjust the position to avoid knots and bark inclusions. When the tracing is positioned correctly, slip carbon paper under it, tape it securely in place, and trace the pattern onto the wood.

DECORATION AND FINISHING

If you are going to tackle carving projects in period styles you need to come to terms with decoration. From the late nineteenth century a kind of 'puritanism' crept into woodcarving which decreed that carvings should have a natural wood finish, perhaps with a little stain or polish. Throughout most periods before the end of the nineteenth century, however, carvings tended to be decorated, and in Georgian times painting and gilding were almost mandatory.

Many of the projects in this book do only require a plain or polished wood finish, but for others you really need to be prepared to go for the appropriate finish to get the true period feel. You will find all the information you need in each of these projects to achieve the type of decorative finish required, but here is a summary of the main techniques.

FUMING OAK

Fuming is used for darkening the colour of oak by exposure to ammonia fumes. It looks more natural than woodstain as it replicates the natural effects of ageing that result from exposure to the air for centuries. With fuming it is possible to condense many centuries of exposure to air into a few hours. By adjusting the amount of time you leave oak in the fumes, you can take it back to Jacobean times (project 6), Tudor times (project 3), or right back to the Dark Ages (project 1). The strong 'household' ammonia – sold as a cleaning fluid by many ironmongers and hardware stores – is the best one to buy. It is safe to use if you follow the manufacturer's safety instructions. Sapwood (the softer outer layer of the tree) does not respond to fuming and will stay pale, so only use fuming on oak heartwood.

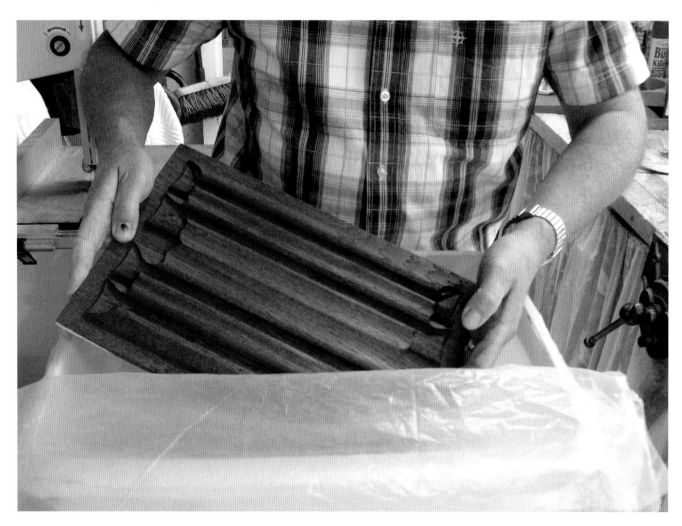

Gilding with Metal Leaf

To a new carver, the prospect of finishing a carving in gold leaf can seem a bit scary, but it is easier than you may think. There are many ways of gilding, and using 'substitute' metal leaf is the simplest. Because the substitute metals are cheaper, the leaf is thicker and easier to handle for a less-experienced user. For a large area of gilding, pure gold can be rather expensive, so the larger projects in this book use imitation gold leaf.

All metals apart from pure gold are liable to tarnish when exposed to air, so they have to be sealed. In this book metal leaf is sealed either with clear artist's varnish or is 'antiqued' with a coat of French polish (a slightly darker version of standard shellac).

Metal leaf is used in projects 2, 11, 13 and 15.

Gilding with Pure Gold Leaf

Some jobs are worth going the extra mile. Gold leaf of 22 to 24 carats is more expensive and a bit harder to handle than imitation gold leaf, but it gives a true gold finish that needs no sealer and will never tarnish. Although more expensive, it is not prohibitively so, especially when used as 'parcel gilding'. 'Parcel', in this context, is a corruption of 'partial' and refers to the practice of gilding parts of a carving as 'highlights', leaving the rest painted, varnished or French polished.

The first time you try gilding with real gold leaf you will find it frustrating but, with a little practice, you should soon get the hang of it. There is nothing quite like real gold for giving a Georgian carving an authentic period look.

$23^3/4$ carat gold leaf is used in projects 14, 16, 17 and 18.

French Polishing

French polish is a solution of shellac in alcohol, which is applied by cloth or brush and built up in thin layers. For most carvings, three to six coats of French polish, applied evenly with a cloth, will give a rich warm colour to the wood and a soft satin gloss to the surface. Mahogany-type woods such as sapele respond best to the colour of French polish.

This combination is used in projects 18 and 19.

TOOLS

I hesitate to specify tools for a particular carving as everyone, including me, has favourite tools that work for them. For each of the 20 projects I have included a photo and description of the tools I used on the carving. It doesn't mean they are the only tools you can use, and it doesn't mean you have to rush out and buy every tool in the picture if you have others that will do the job, but I hope it will show you what tools may be helpful to you.

HAND TOOLS

Power tools can make life easier (as you will see in a few of the projects), but my first choice is usually a traditional gouge or chisel. The picture below illustrates the range of hand tools I used for these projects. If you don't have all these tools, you may be able to get by with the tools you have, and you can gradually add to your collection as you go along. The jigsaw and small handsaws figure greatly in 'pierced' carvings.

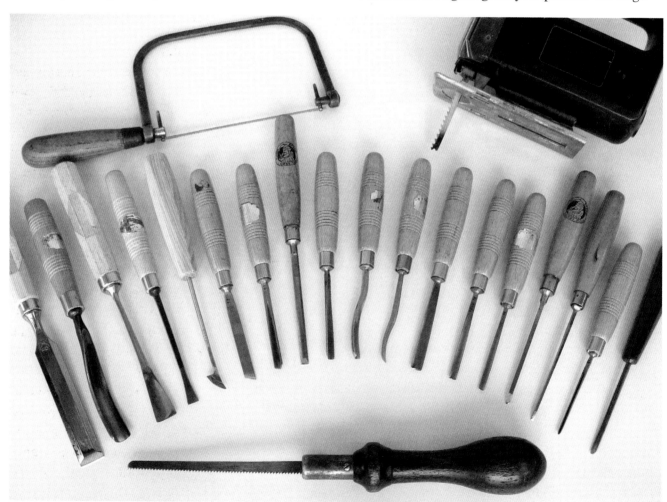

From top left to bottom right:
Coping saw, jigsaw, ^{3}/$_4$in (20mm) flat chisel, ^{5}/$_8$in (16mm) No. 9 curved gouge,
^{3}/$_4$in (20mm) No. 3 fishtail gouge, ^{3}/$_8$in (10mm) No. 3 fishtail gouge, ^{5}/$_8$in (16mm) hooked skew chisel,
^{3}/$_8$in (10mm) skew chisel, V-tool, ^{1}/$_4$in (6mm) fine-ground flat chisel, ^{5}/$_{16}$in (8mm) No. 8 gouge,
^{5}/$_{16}$in (8mm) No. 8 curved gouge, ^{3}/$_{16}$in (5mm) bent chisel, ^{3}/$_8$in (10mm) No. 3 gouge,
^{1}/$_4$in (6mm) No. 5 gouge, ^{3}/$_{16}$in (5mm) No. 5 gouge, ^{1}/$_8$in (3mm) chisel, ^{1}/$_{16}$in (2mm) chisel,
^{1}/$_{16}$in (2mm) No. 11 veiner, ^{3}/$_8$in (3mm) No. 9 gouge, padsaw

MOULDING PLANES

Traditional wooden moulding planes are a useful addition to your toolkit for decorative carving. Try to build up a set of a few concave and convex profiles to help you tackle borders, frames and linenfold panels. They can be a bit difficult to set, having no form of adjustment other than a tap with a hammer, but they are a joy to work with. You will usually need to visit an antique centre to buy them, but you can get new ones from Philly Planes (www.phillyplanes.co.uk).

BANDSAW

A bandsaw is not essential, but it is probably the most useful workshop machine a woodcarver can buy. It will save you hours of sweat and toil over the years. It enables you to cut round the outside of patterns in timber several inches thick, without the problem of flexing you get with a jigsaw. Most projects in this book start with cutting out the pattern on a bandsaw. If you don't have a bandsaw it doesn't mean you can't do it. It just means you will have to work a bit harder with jigsaws and handsaws.

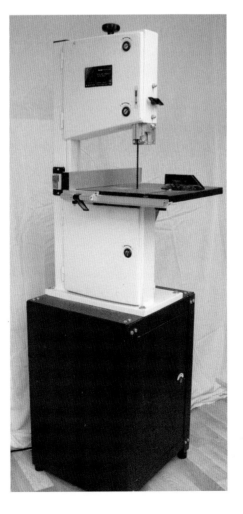

WOODTURNING LATHE

As hobbies, woodcarving and woodturning have rather become separate disciplines, each going their own way, but in a traditional carver's workshop there would have been no clear separation. A woodturning lathe is a very useful tool for a decorative carver, allowing you to expand your carving repertoire significantly.

I have included in this book two projects where a lathe is essential (Projects 11 and 18), and another (Project 13) where a lathe is useful for part of it but not essential. These projects require only a very basic lathe and a few tools, which should not impact too greatly on your budget. The skills required to turn wood can soon be acquired with a little practice (and maybe a book on woodturning), after which you will not only be able to use a lathe to assist your carving but will also have a new hobby of woodturning to fill the gaps between carving projects.

TIMBERS

The projects in this book use mainly two types of timber – oak (*quercus robur*) and lime (*tilia europaea*). These timbers are chosen because they carve well and are easily obtainable.

OAK

Oak has been the timber of choice for carvings from time immemorial. It is attractive, durable and, if used while still 'green', is easy to carve. When you see the words 'green oak' in this book it refers to oak that has been drying in the air for between one and three years from the date of felling. After three years it starts to get progressively harder and more brittle.

Green oak poses a risk that must be balanced against its ease of carving. It is potentially unstable, being prone to unpredictable warping and splitting. You can manage this risk by choosing oak that is straight grained and free from knots. The more contortions it has in the grain, the more likely it is to warp and split. Green oak is not usually stocked by timber merchants or hardwood suppliers (they prefer hard, stable, reliable 8-year-old oak), but you can obtain it from local sawmills, estate foresters and specialist timber suppliers.

Kiln-dried oak is oak that, as the name implies, has been dried artificially in a special kiln. It is a bit harder to carve than green oak, but it reduces the risk of warping so it is the best choice for large flat panels. Life is full of compromises, and there is a trade-off between the extra mallet work involved in using kiln-dried oak and the comfort of knowing it is less likely to twist out of shape after you have finished carving.

LIME/LINDEN

Lime (also known as linden) is the best timber for carving fine detail and thin sections. It was used extensively in the seventeenth and eighteenth centuries, most famously in the limewood foliage carvings of Grinling Gibbons, and is still the most prized carving timber today. It has the close grain of a hardwood (which, technically, it is), but it is soft enough to push a gouge through it with hand pressure.

It cuts cleanly, rarely crumbling at the edges, and retains a high degree of strength even in very thin sections. This is what makes it so ideal for carving leaves and petals with wafer-thin edges. Its American cousin (*tilia americana*) is called basswood and has similar properties.

In its natural state it is not a particularly attractive wood, so it was usually painted and gilded. Although the lime/linden tree is native to Britain and Europe, and basswood to North America, the timber is not widely used for anything other than carving, so you will need to buy it from specialist timber suppliers or, if you are lucky, local sawmills and estate foresters. Estate timber will be cheaper but may have hidden bark inclusions and will need careful drying to avoid shrinkage cracks, so buy more than you need to allow for wastage. Always seal the ends of estate timber with Danish oil, paint, varnish or PVA sealer to reduce the risk of the splitting that occurs when the fibres dry out quicker at the ends than in the middle.

SAPELE

In Georgian and Victorian times, mahogany was the most popular wood for furniture and fittings. It was frequently decorated with carving and turning, to a standard that is remarkable for such a hard wood. It takes French polish particularly well (see projects 18 and 19) and is familiar to all of us as the dark reddish-brown tables and cabinets we see in antique shops. True mahoganies grow in tropical rain forests and, because of environmental sensitivities today, are not easily obtainable. The best substitute available in quantity from ethical sources is sapele (*entandrophragma cylindricum*). It is stocked by specialist hardwood suppliers (look in your local Yellow Pages) but not always by general timber merchants.

There are many more timbers you could use, especially if you live in a part of the world where oak and lime are not native, but as these timbers are most easily available in the northern hemisphere I recommend you use them if you can.

CARVING YOUR WAY THROUGH HISTORY

While this book does not pretend to cover every period style of woodcarving, or indeed to be an academic work on the history of woodcarving, it is helpful to summarize how the projects fit into the stylistic history of European, and particularly British, period decoration. The period divisions are somewhat arbitrary, as they always are, because styles don't change overnight and stylistic periods overlap to a considerable degree. But for convenience I have adopted the traditional practice of dividing periods by their English monarchic dynasties.

450–1066 The Dark Ages

The period from the collapse of Roman Britain in around AD 450 to the Norman invasion of AD 1066 is generally referred to as The Dark Ages – not because it was dark, but because there were few written records to illuminate our knowledge of the period. The Celts, Saxons, and later the Vikings, made the British Isles their own, and it is the intricate knotwork patterns of their jewellery and stone carving that define the artistic style we generally refer to as Celtic.

Project 1 CELTIC CROSS

1066–1485 The Medieval Period

The Medieval period brought us one of the greatest advances in architecture and ornament since the Romans left – the soaring pinnacles, traceried windows and 'grotesque' creatures of Medieval Gothic. Carving abounded in stone and in wood, most of it dedicated to the Glory of God, but only sparsely in domestic houses. The period also brought us another significant development for carvers – Heraldry. Its shields, supporters, crests and mottos have kept carvers employed from the twelfth century to the present day.

LEFT TO RIGHT *Project 2* HERALDIC SHIELD, *Project 7* GOTHIC WINDOW

1485–1603 Tudor and Elizabethan

After the Wars of the Roses (1455–1485) had settled the succession to the throne, Britain entered a period of relative peace, and rich people no longer needed to live in fortified castles. At last, domestic architecture and interior decoration became as great a source of employment for carvers as ecclesiastical carving had been in previous centuries. The gentry were becoming rich and the 'stately home' was born. Walls were covered in wooden panelling. Gothic carving on beams, staircases, doorcases and chimneypieces gradually gave way to strapwork designs, and the Italian Renaissance made a hesitant start in England.

Project 3 TUDOR LINENFOLD PANEL

1603–1714 Jacobean and Stuart

The seventeenth century started when Shakespeare was in his prime, and the theatre was a big influence. The Renaissance finally got into full swing and dominated the first half of the century. The Restoration period (from 1660) was dominated by the Baroque style with its emphasis on 'depth' and 'richness' of carved and painted decoration. Sir Christopher's Wren's rebuilding of London after the Great Fire, and Grinling Gibbons' gravity-defying foliage carvings define the period in Britain.

LEFT TO RIGHT *Project 6* RENAISSANCE OAK PANEL, *Project 20* GRINLING GIBBONS FOLIAGE, *Project 13* ACANTHUS SWIRL

1714–1837 Georgian

The Georgian era covers most of the eighteenth century and the first part of the nineteenth. It is often, and rightly, called 'The Age of Enlightenment' for the rapid advances in science, exploration and learning. As a stylistic era, it covers a wide range of styles from the frivolous curves of Rococo in the early part of the period, to the masculine formality of the Greek Revival in the latter part, passing through the typical Georgian Neo-Classicism we are all familiar with.

LEFT TO RIGHT *Project 15* CHIPPENDALE RIBBON FESTOON, *Project 16* ROCOCO MIRROR FRAME, *Project 18* DOLPHIN TAZZA

'Rococo', also known as Louis XV-style in its French incarnation, followed on from the Baroque. It dominates the magnificent palaces of St Petersburg, Russia, built in the early eighteenth century. The Gothick style (with a 'k') made the first of its comebacks, and Chinoiserie (Chinese style) took the drawing rooms of Britain by storm. Thomas Chippendale published his 'Director' of furniture designs in the Rococo, Classical, Gothick and Chinese styles, driving many carvers to the point of insanity trying to produce them.

LEFT TO RIGHT
Project 12 FRUIT-AND-FLOWER FESTOON, *Project 14* ACANTHUS CRESTING, *Project 17* GEORGIAN CORBEL

1837–1901 Victorian

The Victorian era was a time of rapid change. The old world of rural villages and traditional agriculture was turned on its head by the Industrial Revolution, the growth of cities, railways, steamships and telegraph. The British Empire circled the globe and its influence on foreign cultures was a two-way street. The Great Exhibition of 1851 was one of the first international trade exhibitions, attended not only by the rich and influential, but by the great mass of the expanding population. Design had gone global, and just about every style that had gone before was 'revived' to cater for the ever-expanding market.

LEFT TO RIGHT *Project 11* PUGIN COLUMN TABLE, *Project 9* THE DRAGON OF EYE

The greatest of the Victorian revivals was the Gothic Revival (without a 'k') led by A. W. N. Pugin – a purer and more polychrome Medieval Gothic than the eighteenth- century 'Gothick'. Its influence spread around the world, particularly to North America and Australia. There was another Neo-Classical Revival, a Jacobean Revival, a Neo-Renaissance and a Neo-Baroque. The Italianate style became the main competitor for Gothic. Byzantine and Venetian ornament had a strong influence with their Arabesque vines and Islamic arches. One of the few truly Victorian styles was the abundant use of flowers and foliage.

LEFT TO RIGHT *Project 5* HOLKER OLIVE PANEL, *Project 10* ST IVES FOLIAGE PANEL, *Project 19* LARGE-SCALE ARABESQUE

1901–1910 Edwardian

The Edwardian period could be seen as just an extension of the Victorian era, but the turn of a new century brought new influences. The Victorian 'revival' styles still dominated, but Gothic began to decline. In Britain, a simpler style developed under the influence of the Arts and Crafts Movement. Starting in late-Victorian times, it was a reaction against industrial mass-production, celebrating traditional materials, traditional methods and, above all, the skill of the craftsman. With education and evening classes promoting 'self-betterment' for the masses, it led many a worker into the hobby of woodcarving.

But the twentieth-century world also wanted something new and dynamic, and it came from Europe – Art Nouveau – the 'New Art'. This was the style of mass-production. It quickly spread across Europe and America to become a global style. It flowered until the Great War of 1914–18 snuffed it out, like so much else.

ABOVE *Project 4* ARTS AND CRAFTS FLOWER PANEL, BELOW *Project 8* THE PEACOCK OF RIGA

The
PROJECTS

Project 1

CELTIC CROSS

The Celtic cross is an evocative symbol of Britain's ancient past, conjuring up images of mist-shrouded monasteries on rocky headlands, battered by waves and pillaged by Vikings in the period known by the sinister name of 'The Dark Ages'.

When the Romans left Britain in AD 410 their nascent Christianity quickly faded and the Celts slipped back into their old paganism – but not for long. By about AD 650 saintly missionaries from Rome started arriving to convert the ancient Celts and the Saxon newcomers from their pagan ways. These conversions were not completely successful because old habits die hard. Their old religion had a rich decorative vocabulary of evocative symbols and elaborate knotwork, which they found hard to discard. So, in a spirit of compromise, they simply 'recycled' the symbols of the old faith into their new one, creating the mysterious and spiritual crosses that are the most enduring symbol of Celtic art.

The missionary bishops of the Dark Ages were fairly pragmatic about reusing the symbols and festivities of the old religions if it made the transition easier, so in this spirit I have allowed more than a touch of 'sorcery' to creep into this design. As well as a 'trinity knot', it includes a star, a crescent moon and a four-sided pyramid representing 'earth, air, fire and water'.

To give the carving a real feel of the Dark Ages you can blacken the oak by the process of 'fuming' with ammonia. This is very easy to do. It replicates the natural process of ageing, but at the rate of about a century an hour. In fact, in a few hours it will look so old you will have trouble convincing people you have just made it!

SCALE DRAWING OF THE CELTIC CROSS PATTERN ON A 1IN (25MM) GRID. ENLARGE THE DRAWING TO THE REQUIRED SIZE.

450–1066 The Dark Ages

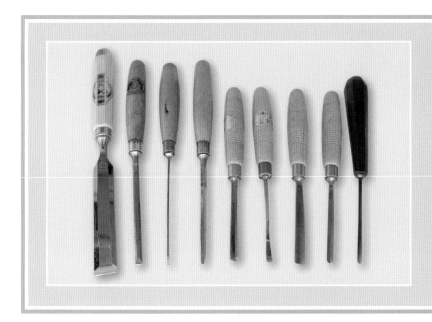

TOOLS AND MATERIALS

Wood: Oak (*quercus robur*),
13 x 7 x ³/₄in (330 x 178 x 18mm)

Tools, *from left to right:*
³/₄in (20mm) flat chisel, ¹/₄in (6mm)
fine-ground flat chisel, ¹/₁₆in (2mm)
chisel, ¹/₈in (3mm) chisel, V-tool,
³/₁₆in (5mm) bent chisel, ³/₈in (10mm)
No. 3 gouge, ¹/₄in (6mm) No. 5 gouge,
¹/₈in (3mm) No. 9 gouge

Finishing materials: Household
ammonia (for fuming), good-quality
furniture polish

SHAPING THE CROSS

1 Make a full-size copy of the drawing and trace it onto a piece of green oak, 13 x 7 x ³/₄in (330 x 178 x 18mm), using carbon paper. If you intend to fume it later, make sure your oak is all heartwood and doesn't have any sapwood in it, as sapwood (the softer new growth on the outer edge of the tree) will not darken when fumed.

2 Cut around the outside of the pattern with a bandsaw or jigsaw, and trim up the edges to a smooth finish with a spokeshave and a flat chisel. Use a jigsaw with a ³/₁₆in (5mm) 'scroll' blade, or a coping saw, to cut out the sections inside the ring.

3 Fix the cross to a backing board by screwing from the back with two short screws, and clamp the board to the bench. Cut the surface of the 'ring of eternity' down to ¹/₄in (6mm) below the surface of the cross with a flat chisel.

CARVING THE KNOTWORK AND SYMBOLS

4 Draw two lines ³/₁₆in (5mm) in from the inner and outer edges of the ring, leaving a ³/₁₆in (5mm) strip in the middle. Cut a U-shaped cove along this strip with a ¹/₈in (3mm) No. 9 gouge, taking care to keep the cutting edge on the 'downstream' side of the grain in each direction.

6 Mark the overlaps on the knotwork, then work them down so the 'ribbons' appear to flow smoothly over and under one another without disappearing into the background.

5 Start by using a V-tool to cut around the pattern lines to define the edges. Don't be tempted to 'bost' down vertically just yet as the pressure may break out parts of the pattern. The thin cross-grain sections of the pattern are particularly vulnerable to break-out. With the V-cuts relieving the pressure, you can then make the edges vertical with paring and 'bosting' cuts using fine chisels. Take particular care with the outer border. You can clamp a steel rule along the straight edges to give you a clean straight cut. Cut away the background areas to about ³/₁₆in (5mm) below the top surface. There are some very narrow gaps, so you will need chisels as small as ¹/₁₆in (2mm) in width.

7 Use a No. 5 gouge to carve the central 'trinity' knot so the three rounded strands seem to wrap into one another like an endless cord. To carve the star, create angular faces with a flat chisel, taking great care with grain direction. Try to get good sharp edges as the shadows will define the shape.

8 To carve the crescent moon, scoop out a hollow on the right-hand side with a No. 5 gouge to leave a crescent on the left side. Give the inside of the crescent a sharp edge to create a strong shadow, and round over the outward side. The four-sided symbol (representing earth, air, fire and water) is carved using a flat chisel, cutting from the centre down towards each of the four edges.

FINISHING OFF THE CARVING

BACK TO THE DARK AGES

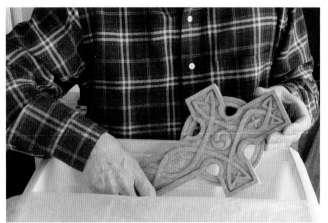

10 Fuming with ammonia is the traditional way of darkening oak. It looks more natural than stains because it causes the same chemical changes in the wood's natural tannins as ageing does. It effectively compresses the chemical changes of centuries into a few hours. Fuming is easy – you just need some sort of container that you can make airtight with the wood inside it, such as this plastic tub. Pour four or five tablespoons of household ammonia (see page 10) into the bottom of the container. Place the cross clear of the bottom on a couple of wooden supports, allowing the fumes to flow freely around the wood. Cover and seal the tub.

9 If you want to leave the cross in its natural 'new' colour and you don't intend to fume it, you can give it a coat of wax polish to bring up the natural colour. However, if you have decided to go the 'full Celtic', don't put anything on the surface just yet.

11 The time taken for fuming depends on a number of variables (strength and volume of ammonia, temperature, and the darkness you want to achieve), so it is more of an art than a science. The cross should take 12 to 24 hours to go from 'pale and interesting' to 'dark and mysterious'. If it is too slow to darken, add more ammonia and leave it a few hours more. Give the raised pattern a rub over with a good wax furniture polish, leaving the background unpolished for contrast. Now hang it on the wall, and try to convince people you haven't found it on an archaeological dig.

Celtic

Project 2
HERALDIC SHIELD

*In days of old, when knights were bold, it was difficult to tell one from
the other on the battlefield as they were all dressed from head to toe in armour.
So, the 'coat of arms' was invented to give each man a distinctive
visual identity by which he could be recognized as friend or foe.*

This shield is a fairly simple carving project, which introduces you to some decorative techniques that will stand you in good stead for other more complex projects. Many carvers are uncomfortable with the idea of painting and gilding their carvings, and for the last hundred years or more there has been a puritanical notion that all carvings should display the 'beauty of the wood'. While this is true of some carvings, it is a false notion where much decorative carving is concerned, and particularly so with heraldic carving. A heraldic shield without colour is an oxymoron. A 'coat of arms' is defined by a *blazon* which prescribes its colours as much as the objects it includes.

The shield I have designed for this project is based on a variant of the old French royal arms as quartered on the arms of the kings of England from 1340 (when Edward III laid claim to the throne of France) until 1801 (when George III finally let it go). I have added a chevron as a 'difference' (a heraldic term) purely for decorative effect, although such a difference could well have been used by a subsidiary branch of the French royal house.

The blazon (description) for this shield would be: *Azure, a chevron argent, three fleurs-de-lys or.* This translates as a silver chevron and gold fleurs-de-lys on a blue shield. If you think that is complicated, it gets much worse after the medieval period when 'armigerous' families intermarried and 'quartered' their arms together on their shields, gradually building up more quarterings as the generations went on. A prominent family could soon achieve their *seize quartiers* (sixteen quarters – the mark of true nobility), and by the nineteenth century 32 quarters and more would not be uncommon. That is why I have stuck to a medieval shield – you really don't want to start with the Victorian aristocracy!

1066–1485 The Medieval Period

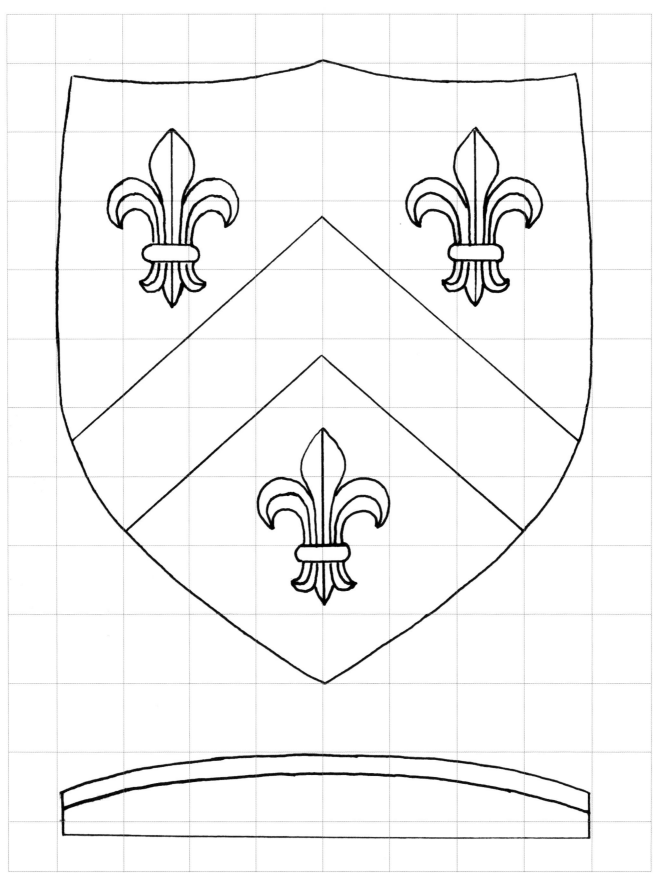

SCALE DRAWING OF THE HERALDIC SHIELD PATTERN ON A 1IN (25MM) GRID. ENLARGE THE DRAWING TO THE REQUIRED SIZE.

1066–1485 The Medieval Period

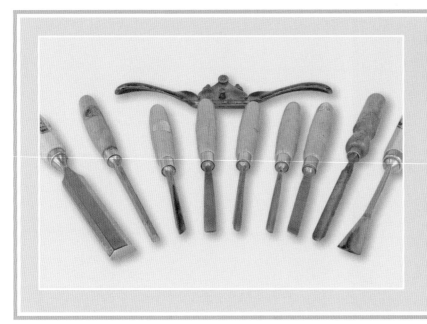

TOOLS AND MATERIALS

Wood: Lime (*tilia* spp),
8 x 9 x 1¹/₄in (203 x 229 x 32mm)

Tools, *from top and left to right:* spokeshave,
³/₄in (20mm) flat chisel, ¹/₄in (6mm)
fine-ground flat chisel, V-tool, (10mm)
No. 3 gouge, ⁵/₁₆in (8mm) No. 8 gouge,
¹/₄in (6mm) No. 5 gouge, ¹/₄in (10mm)
skew chisel, ³/₈in (10mm) No. 8 gouge,
³/₄in (20mm) No. 3 fishtail gouge

Finishing materials: Danish Oil (sealer),
grey primer, blue acrylic paint, imitation
silver leaf, imitation gold leaf, gilding size,
artist's clear varnish

SHAPING THE SHIELD

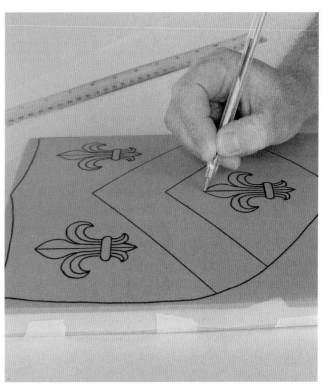

1 Start the project with a piece of wood 8 x 9 x 1¹/₄in (203 x 229 x 32mm). Any suitable carving wood will do, but here I've used lime as it is the easiest to carve. Appearance is not an issue as the lime will be decorated. Mark a line on each end of the wood, going in a smooth curve from the 1¹/₄in (32mm) thickness in the middle down to ³/₄in (19mm) at the edges. Plane the surface of the wood down to these lines to create the curved surface of the shield. Get a good finish as part of this surface will form the chevron.

2 Make a full-size copy of the drawing and trace it onto the planed curved surface using carbon paper. Line the drawing up carefully and fix it in place with masking tape so it doesn't wander while you are tracing.

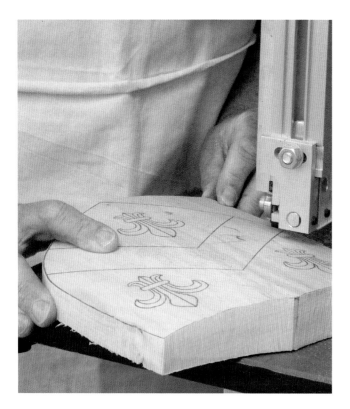

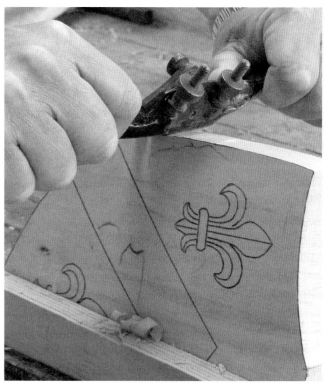

3 Cut around the edge of the shield using a bandsaw or coping saw (it is difficult to use a jigsaw because of the curved face).

4 Smooth the edges with a spokeshave.

5 Draw two lines all the way around the edges, working from the face side. One line should be ¹/₄in (6mm) from the face, and the other should be ³/₄in (19mm) from the face. The ¹/₂in (13mm) gap between these two lines will be the finished edge of the shield.

6 Using a spokeshave or a flat chisel, shave away some wood at the back of the shield to slope the flat underside up to the back edge of the shield (the lower of the two lines). The idea of this is so that, viewed from the front or sides, the shield will appear to be curved both front and back.

CARVING THE DETAIL

7 Fix the shield to a larger board for carving so you can clamp it to the bench. Either screw through from the back with two short screws or, as I have done here, use self-adhesive Velcro tape. Cut around the edges of the pattern with a V-tool to separate the detail from the 'ground'.

8 Use a medium-sized gouge to rough out the surplus wood in the 'ground'. Be careful not to go below the ¹/₄in (6mm) level that will be the background surface of the shield. A gouge is better than a flat chisel for roughing out as its U-shape takes in the sides of the cut as well as the bottom, giving you more control.

9 With the surplus wood removed you can 'bost' around the pattern to give it clean edges. Use gouges with the right curve to make vertical cuts around the fleurs-de-lys. The chevron needs to have good straight edges. Clamping a ruler firmly to the carving will give a good edge to place your chisel against – much better than working freehand.

10 Smooth off the ground with a shallow fishtail gouge and a flat chisel. Bring the surface down level with the ¹/₄in (6mm) line at the edge, and check that the edges of the chevron and fleurs-de-lys are ¹/₄in (6mm) deep.

11 There is not much 'modelling' of shapes in this carving, but we have now come to it. Shape the fleurs-de-lys firstly by using a V-tool to separate the three 'stems' of the lily. Use a fine flat chisel to put a chamfer on the straight and convex sides of the stems, and a No. 5 to No. 8 gouge to chamfer the concave turns. Slightly round over the edges and ends of the 'band' holding the three stems together.

Medieval Heraldry

12 Remove any stringy bits with the point of a skew chisel, and finish the carving by putting a chamfer on the ends of the chevron so they are distinct from the edges of the shield. Sand the edges and background with 240-grit abrasive to get a good surface. Give the fleurs-de-lys a very light sanding if necessary, taking care to keep the carving crisp. Here is the finished carving, looking a bit pale until some colour is brought into its life.

PAINTING AND GILDING

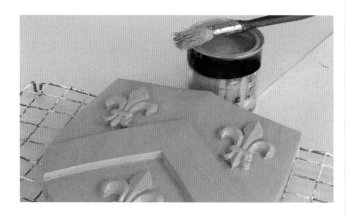

13 Seal the wood with a coat of Danish oil and let it dry overnight (always remember to do any board both sides, otherwise it will curl as one side dries and shrinks more than the other). Give the whole front surface of the shield a coat of grey primer. Take care not to get paint on the sides of the shield, and do not clog the detail on the fleurs-de-lys with too much paint.

14 Give the main surface of the shield one or two coats of blue acrylic paint, again taking care at the edges. If you are new to gilding it is best to give the fleurs-de-lys a coat of gold lacquer and the chevron a coat of silver lacquer. This will provide an undercoat for the metal leaf so the inevitable tears and gaps in the gilding will not show as much. If you don't want to use gilding, you could leave the shield with just the lacquered decoration, but the finish will not be quite as good.

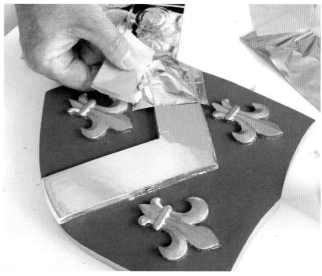

15 If you are ready to tackle gilding, apply a coat of gilding size to the chevron and leave it about 15 minutes to become touch-dry but slightly tacky. Apply silver (aluminium) leaf to the surface and the vertical edges. This takes a bit of practice but you will soon master it. Because the chevron is large and flat, you can use a quarter of a sheet at a time. Overlap the pieces as you go until you have covered the whole chevron. Use a soft brush to press it down and brush away loose pieces. Go over any bare patches with more leaf.

16 Repeat this process on the fleurs-de-lys using imitation gold leaf (you could use genuine gold but it is harder to handle if you are new to this, and it is a lot more expensive). You will find the fleurs-de-lys a bit trickier as the metal leaf tends to fall apart in the V between each stem, so apply the leaf in small pieces.

17 Unlike genuine gold leaf, imitation gold and silver leaf will tarnish if left exposed to the air for long, so give the metal a coat of clear artist's varnish to seal it. Now hang your shield somewhere you can admire it. The Edwardians loved to have them all around the room just below ceiling level, especially in the great hall and billiard room. I don't have a great hall or billiard room, so I'll stick with just the one shield.

HERALDRY IN CARVING

Heraldry and decorative carving are very closely linked. You can make a heraldic carving as simple or as complex as you wish, from a simple shield like this project, to a full 'achievement of arms' including shield, supporters, helm, crest and motto.

Heraldry is a fascinating subject that is well worth the attention of a decorative carver. It has complex and fascinating rules and its own language (Norman French), which it has retained since the twelfth century. It has strict rules about colour, which you need to be aware of when you do a heraldic carving. There are only five colours, two 'metals' and two 'furs' which, with their old Norman French names, are:

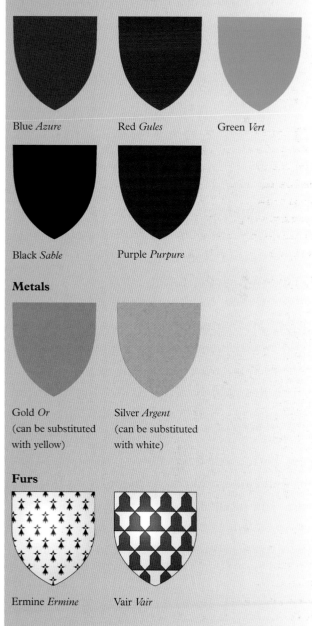

Blue *Azure* Red *Gules* Green *Vert*

Black *Sable* Purple *Purpure*

Metals

Gold *Or*
(can be substituted
with yellow)

Silver *Argent*
(can be substituted
with white)

Furs

Ermine *Ermine* Vair *Vair*

Project 3

TUDOR LINENFOLD PANEL

*When Henry Tudor defeated Richard III at Bosworth Field in 1485 and became
King Henry VII, the medieval period came to an end and the Tudor period began.
The Tudor age (1485–1603) spawned some of England's bloodiest monarchs,
but it also marked a transition from the cold and draughty castles of
the medieval period to the beginnings of 'the stately homes of England'.*

In Tudor times the upwardly mobile gentry were becoming rich by commerce and agriculture – especially the wool trade. With the 'peace dividend' from the conclusion of the Wars of the Roses, they no longer needed to live in fortified castles and wanted comfortable grand houses befitting their new station in life. Stone walls were out – linenfold panelling was in.

The linenfold pattern, as the name suggests, represents the folds of a piece of linen fabric. It developed in late medieval times, probably as a more permanent alternative to the fabrics with which chamber walls were draped to make them more comfortable. It was used extensively as 'wainscot' to panel walls, as well as on doors and chests. It is the quintessential decorative feature of the Tudor period, and enjoyed a huge renaissance during Victorian and Edwardian times.

Although linenfold panels are not made exclusively from oak, it is the traditional material for them. Oak is durable, attractive, available, and it carves well. For us, it also has the advantage that it can be aged to look more ancient than it is by the process of 'fuming' with ammonia. Fuming is simple, as you will have seen if you tackled Project 1.

You may not want to go so far as panelling a room with wainscot, but linenfold is ideal for panelling a wooden chest or for enhancing doors (you could try Tudor kitchen cupboards or wardrobes). As in this case, it also makes an attractive and even ancient-looking decorative panel, just to hang on a wall.

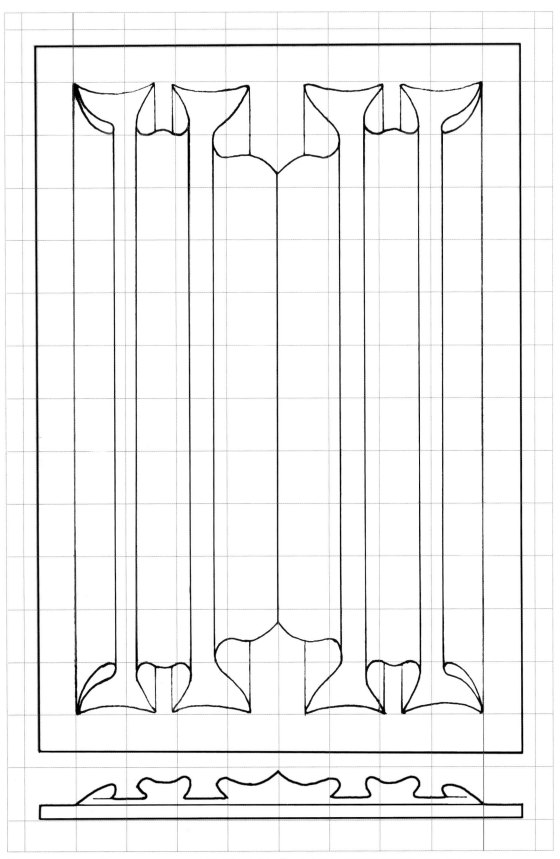

SCALE DRAWING OF THE LINENFOLD PATTERN ON A 1IN (25MM) GRID. ENLARGE THE DRAWING TO THE REQUIRED SIZE.

1485–1603 Tudor and Elizabethan

TOOLS AND MATERIALS

Wood: Oak (*quercus robur*),
13¼ x 9½ x ⅞in (343 x 241 x 22mm)

Tools, *from left to right:*
Planes: ½in (13mm) convex moulding
plane, 1in (25mm) convex moulding
plane, ½in (13mm) concave moulding
plane, plough/rebate plane.
Chisels and gouges: ¼in (6mm) fine-
ground flat chisel, ⅜in (10mm) No. 3
gouge, ¼in (6mm) No. 5 gouge, V-tool

Finishing materials: Household
ammonia (for fuming), good-quality
wax polish

PREPARATIONS

1 Make a full-size copy of the pattern and trace it onto a
piece of oak about ⅞in (22mm) thick. If the panel is to be
fitted into a chest, door, or wainscot framework, the outer ¼in
(6mm) of the border will be covered by the framework. You can
make the drawing fit the width of a specific frame, and extend
the lengthways lines as required. It is easier to work on if you
fix it to a backing board (self-adhesive Velcro is very effective),
which you can clamp to the bench.

PLANING THE GROOVES

2 Cut a rebate on each of the long sides with a rebate plane.
Take it down to a ¼in (6mm) thickness at the edges (we
will call this the base level). Next, use a plough plane to cut the
channels between the folds. Take these down to ⅛in (3mm)
above the base level to form the 'ground' for the linenfold (we
will call this the ground level to avoid confusion with the base
level). Cutting the channels is easier if you use a tenon saw to
cut down to depth just inside the guide lines, then chisel out
some of the waste before bringing the plough plane into use.

Tudor Style

3 Use convex and concave moulding planes to form the 'folds'. Make sure you form a sharp 'crease' in the central fold. If you don't have moulding planes you can do the job by careful use of gouges. To undercut the folds where they meet the ground in the channels, lay a tenon saw on its side and run it along the edge, then round off the underside with a gouge.

CARVING THE ENDS

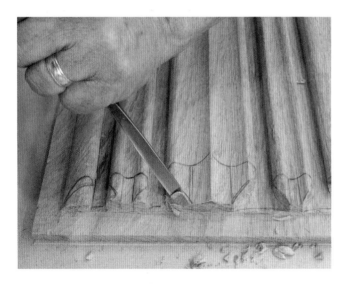

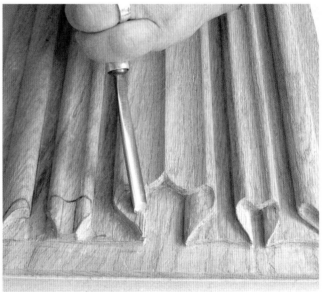

4 With the lengthways pattern formed it is time to tackle the ends. First cut across the folds ³/₄in (19mm) from the ends and plane down to the base level. Draw the end pattern back on (it was planed off when making the folds). We now switch from planes to carving tools. Use a shallow gouge and a fine flat chisel to cut away the corners at the ends of the folds down to the ground of the linen, about ¹/₈in (3mm) above the base level.

5 Still using a shallow gouge and a fine flat chisel, cut out the centre channel in the end of each fold down to the base level. Where the pattern curves across the top of the fold, cut down vertically about halfway, then round the reverse folds down into the channel. Undercut the edges and round the folds so it looks like a piece of fabric folded and laying on top of the base board. Finally, shape the line where the bottom of the folds meets the base rebate, so it curves slightly from one fold to the next. The end pattern is the defining feature of the whole linenfold, so try to get a nice smooth flow and clean sharp edges.

1485–1603 **Tudor and Elizabethan**

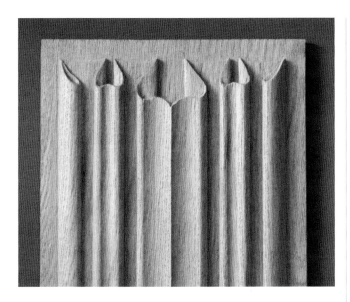

6 With the ends carved we are nearly finished. To keep the piece looking crisp, avoid using abrasives. A good tooled finish will give it more life and have more of a period look. However, you may have noticed that this oak is looking a little pale compared to the dark brown colour we are used to seeing on Tudor linenfold. If you want your Tudor panel to look more authentic, you can use wood stains (acceptable, but not entirely natural looking), or you can start fuming.

FUMING

7 Fuming with ammonia is the traditional way of darkening oak. It effectively compresses the chemical changes of centuries into a few hours. Fuming is easy – you just need some sort of tent or container that you can make airtight with the wood inside it, such as this plastic tub. I am using polythene sheet to cover the top, sealed around the edges with double-sided tape. Pour a few tablespoons of ammonia into a saucer or into the bottom of the tub. Place the panel clear of the bottom on a couple of wooden supports, allowing the fumes to flow freely around it. Cover and seal the tub.

8 After about 12 hours, remove the panel from the fuming box. It should be a nice deep brown. The time taken for fuming depends on a number of variables (strength and volume of ammonia, temperature, and the darkness you want to achieve), so it is more of an art than a science. Check the colour every few hours and take the panel out when it looks about right. If it is too slow to darken, add more ammonia and leave it a few hours more.

9 When the panel is fumed, it will have aged centuries in a day and will look like the real thing. Give it a rub over with a good wax furniture polish. Now you can hang your panel on the wall as a decoration, or make some more like it to panel a door, a chest, or even a room.

Project 4

ARTS AND CRAFTS FLOWER PANEL

The Arts and Crafts Movement in the late nineteenth and early twentieth centuries was, as the name implies, as much an ethos as a style. In an age where mass-production was churning out cheap machine-made goods to furnish the Victorian and Edwardian home, the Arts and Crafts Movement stood up for traditional values in design and craftsmanship. It celebrated the skill of the artisan and the dignity of manual labour. It was, if you like, the craftsperson's 'Jerusalem' – an evangelical reaction against the 'dark satanic mills' of industrialization.

Arts and Crafts can be a hard style to pin down. In the architecture of Philip Webb and Edwin Lutyens its keynotes are traditional materials, simplicity of design and solidity of construction. The same attributes are found in the furniture of the period. But in internal decoration, such as the wallpapers of William Morris, it often takes on an altogether more floral look. Stylized flowers and foliage covered the walls, curtains and, in particular, the carvings of late Victorian and Edwardian rooms.

The design for this panel was inspired by Blackwell – a well-known Arts and Crafts house in the English Lake District designed by Mackay Hugh Ballie Scott (1865–1945).

Built in 1900, with magnificent views over Windermere, it has some superb oak panelling carved in the Arts and Crafts style. Most of this is too complex for a simple carving project, but a tulip motif on the stained-glass windows encapsulated the spirit of the style and provided the basis for this panel.

In stylistic terms, Arts and Crafts is a close relative of Art Nouveau, and in this panel I have employed some of the distinctive period features. The hollow in the broadest leaf, the flattening of the tulip flower, and the angular double-bend at the 'root' end of the stem are features typical of the style. What makes this panel more Arts and Crafts than Art Nouveau is the simplicity of the design and the comparative solidity of the oak.

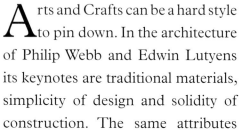

1901–1910 **Edwardian**

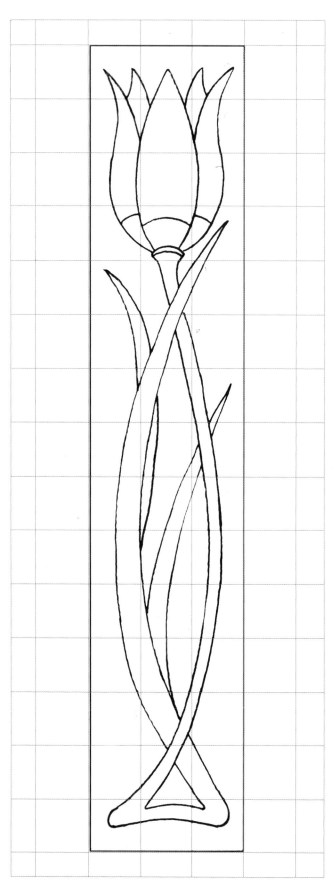

SCALE DRAWING OF THE ARTS AND CRAFTS PATTERN ON A 1IN (25MM) GRID. ENLARGE THE DRAWING TO THE REQUIRED SIZE.

1901–1910 Edwardian

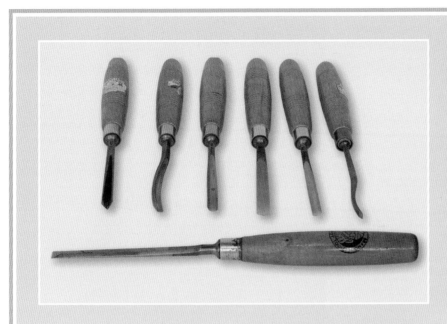

TOOLS AND MATERIALS

Wood: Oak (*quercus robur*), 15 x 3 x 1¹/₄in (381 x 76 x 30mm)

Tools, *from left to right:* ¹/₄in (6mm) fine-ground flat chisel, V-tool, ⁵/₁₆in (8mm) No. 8 curved gouge, ⁵/₁₆in (8mm) No. 8 gouge, ³/₈in (10mm) No. 3 gouge, ¹/₄in (6mm) No. 5 gouge, ¹/₄in (6mm) bent chisel.

Finish: A good-quality wax polish

PREPARATION

1 Make a full-size copy of the pattern. Get a piece of oak 15 x 3 x 1¹/₄in (381 x 76 x 30mm) and some carbon paper. 'Green' oak (oak that has been air-drying for less than three years) is much easier to carve than fully dried oak, so try to get some from an estate forester, a local sawmill, or a specialist supplier.

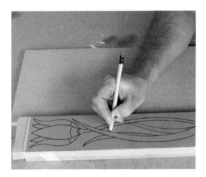

2 Trace the pattern onto the block, making sure your tracing is securely taped to the wood to avoid it wandering. Mark a line around the sides of the block ¹/₂in (13mm) from the top. This will be the 'ground' level for the carving.

SETTING IN AND GROUNDING OUT

3 Fix the wood to a backing board (for clamping to the bench) and define the edges of the pattern with a V-tool. Do not 'bost' down vertically at this stage, as you will create ragged and fractured edges.

TIP: GREEN OAK

Oak was the dominant wood for Arts and Crafts carving. Ideally you need 'green' oak which has been drying for a couple of years, as it is easier to carve than fully dried oak. The only drawback is its tendency to warp as it continues to dry out, so avoid pieces with knots or a contorted grain pattern. On a panel of this size any later warping should not be too pronounced.

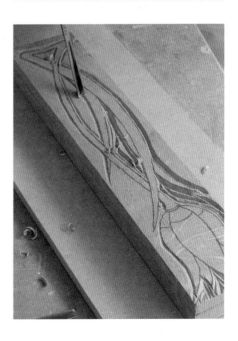

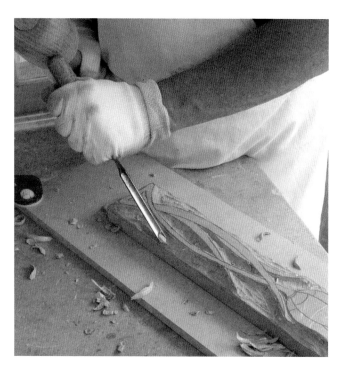

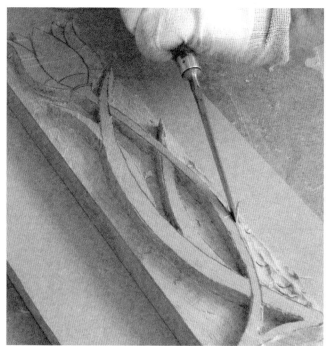

4 Cut away the bulk of the waste wood with a stout gouge and mallet to just above the 'ground'.

5 Square up the vertical edges of the pattern by paring along the sides with a fine flat chisel, always working with the grain.

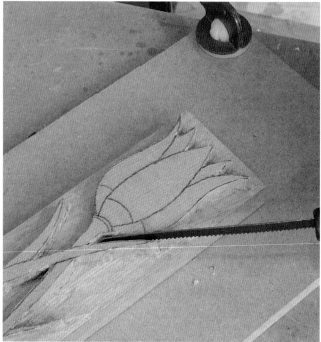

6 In certain areas, like external points and internal corners, you will need to refine the paring cuts by careful vertical 'bosting' cuts. Your tools need to be sharp for this so you don't crush the grain and break off the points. Thin slices with a sharp tool will avoid this problem.

7 The narrow gap between the top of the main leaf and the flower is best tackled with a padsaw – don't attempt to chisel it out at this stage. With the plant form now clearly defined, use a broader chisel to flatten off the ground. You don't need to be too fussy, as we will texture the ground later.

1901–1910 **Edwardian**

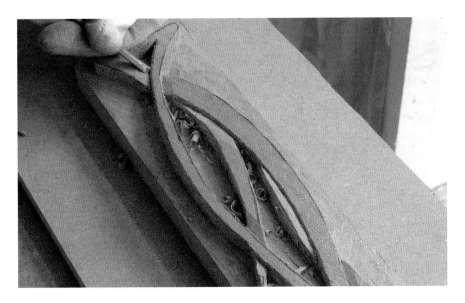

MOULDING THE STEM AND LEAVES

8 Start carving the stem and leaves by defining the overlaps at the crossing points. See how the stem goes over the main leaf at the root end, and under it at the flower end. The two subsidiary leaves flow out from under the main leaf – one crossing under it to the left, and the other crossing under the stem to the right.

9 Shape the stem and leaves, mainly with the concave side of No. 3 and No. 5 gouges. Where leaves and stems cross over and under one another, make sure the line and profile continue on each side of the crossover without any jarring changes in direction. Also make sure the rise and fall above the ground is smooth and natural. Try to capture the period style when you form the hollows in the main leaf and the 'root'.

10 Undercut the leaves and stem so they appear to be appliquéd onto the board. Because the detail and background are the same colour, undercutting is needed to create shadows to separate them visually. First 'undermine' the vertical edge with a V-tool, then open out the undercut with gouges.

Arts and Crafts

SHAPING THE FLOWER

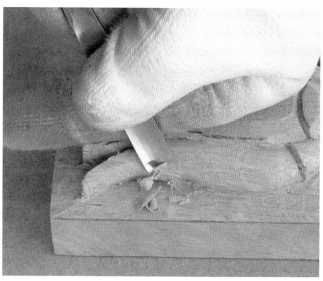

11 Define the overlaps of the flower petals by making a shallow cut with a V-tool on the lower side of each line. Make the two small petal points slope back under the three main petals, but leave their tips at the original level.

12 Use a No. 3 gouge to round over the two side petals, with their inner edges slightly undercutting the centre petal. The change in grain direction in the neck of the curve can make it difficult to get a clean cut. Pare in from each direction, then shave down vertically to get a clean finish in the bend.

13 Shape the centre petal by running a groove down each side with a No. 5 gouge, so the edges of the petal appear to flip up and over the side petals. This is very much a style of this period and getting it right is an important part of the period detail. Round the central part of the petal smoothly into the side hollows.

14 The three centre points of the petals need very pronounced undercutting so they appear fully detached from the ground. This is an illusion achieved by leaving about 1/4in (6mm) thickness at the edges and cutting back below that at an angle of about 45 degrees. The longitudinal grain means the points are quite strong, but don't shave them too thin.

TEXTURING THE GROUND

15 To help the pattern stand out from the ground, texture the ground surface to give a contrast. Using a ⁵/₁₆in (8mm) No. 8 curved gouge or similar, reduce the ground down to its final level with lots of little 'scooping' cuts. Give your cuts a natural directional flow to simulate background grass and foliage, using the flow of the leaves and stem as your guide.

FINISHING TOUCHES

16 One final touch is to put a cove (with a moulding plane) or a chamfer (with a small, flat plane) along each edge of the panel. Always plane across the end grain first, taking care not to break out the corners. It helps if you clamp a piece of wood alongside the panel to keep the plane level and stop it slipping off the edge.

17 Finally, polish the whole panel with a good, light-brown wax polish and hang it on the wall where the light strikes it obliquely.

Arts and Crafts

Project 5

HOLKER OLIVE PANEL

Fire was a great destroyer of period buildings. With heating provided by open fires, and light provided by burning candles, it is little wonder that most historic buildings have been the victims of fire at some point in their history. But, just as a cloud has a silver lining, a fire can often be a catalyst for the creation of something new and even better than what was there before.

When the Victorian owners of Holker Hall, a historic house on the edge of the English Lake District, rebuilt the west wing after a devastating fire in 1871, they decided to stick with oak panelling. But, wanting to modernize at the same time, they decorated the panelling in a new and unmistakably Victorian style. In so doing, they created rooms that are a woodcarver's delight, and well worth a visit if you are in the area.

To execute this new plan of decoration they not only used oak grown on their own estate, but also employed local craftsmen to carve it. The quality of the resulting carving vindicates this decision.

The panels they created are mainly based on foliage, some of which is stylized and some is entirely natural. My eye was caught by a panel carved with what appears to be a natural olive-branch pattern – possibly this symbolizes peace or perhaps, like me, they just thought it looked nice. With the help of a sympathetic room warden, I took notes and turned them into what I hope is a fairly accurate rendering of this design.

The panel is a bas-relief ('bas' is simply French for 'low'). The pattern is raised just $1/4$in (6mm) above the background, giving the effect of a 'picture' in wood. To enhance this effect I have given the panel a 'picture frame' that is moulded into the panel itself. The frame will test your skill at carving straight lines, but it is easier than making up a separate frame with all the problems of cutting rebates and mitres.

In carving this, I hope you will be inspired by the local Victorian craftsmen of Holker, whose carvings rose, phoenix-like, from the ashes of disaster.

1837–1901 **Victorian**

SCALE DRAWING OF THE VICTORIAN OLIVE PATTERN ON A 1IN (25MM) GRID. ENLARGE THE DRAWING TO THE REQUIRED SIZE.

1837–1901 Victorian

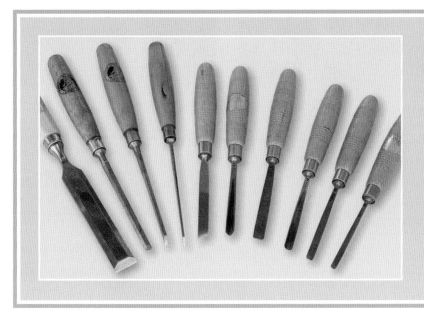

TOOLS AND MATERIALS

Wood: 'Green' oak (*quercus robur*), $8^1/2$ x $11^1/2$ x $^3/4$in (216 x 292 x 19mm)

Tools (*from left to right*): $^3/4$in (20mm) flat chisel, $^1/4$in (6mm) fine-ground flat chisel, $^1/8$in (3mm) chisel, $^1/16$in (2mm) chisel, $^3/8$in (10mm) skew chisel, V-tool, $^3/8$in (10mm) No. 3 gouge, $^5/16$in (8mm) No. 8 gouge, $^1/4$in (6mm) No. 5 gouge, $^3/16$in (5mm) No. 5 gouge

Finish: A good-quality wax polish

PREPARATIONS

1 Start by tracing the pattern onto a board of green oak $8^1/2$ x $11^1/2$ x $^3/4$in (216 x 292 x 19 mm). I used green oak because it carves easier, but it is a fairly thin board, so you need to be confident it will not warp or split. Choose a board that is fairly straight-grained and free from knots. Check that the end grain does not show a radial curve as this makes warping more likely. Keep the board indoors for a few weeks to see how it behaves. If it starts to curl, try another piece or, if necessary, use kiln-dried oak which will be a bit harder to carve but less likely to warp.

CARVING THE FRAME

2 Begin carving by marking out the straight internal edge of the integral frame, and the outer edge of the olive pattern. Clamp a steel rule along the inner edge of the frame and use this to guide a broad flat chisel. Cut down just a fraction at a time – any more would crush and split the fibres and give you a rough edge. Use a V-tool, a No. 8 gouge, $^1/8$in (3mm) and $^1/16$in (2mm) flat chisels to 'ground out' the surface between the olive leaves, and frame down to a depth of $^1/4$in (6mm).

Victorian Foliage

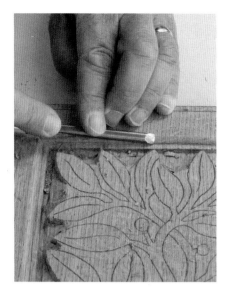

3 Now make a 'step' around the inner edge of the frame, at a depth and width of ¹/₈in (3mm), using the steel rule as before. This will test your ability to cut straight and level by hand with a small flat chisel. Shape the inner moulding of the integral frame with the concave side of a No. 5 gouge. Make sure you get a clean mitre at the corners.

CARVING THE PATTERN

6 'Block out' the rest of the olive pattern to a depth of ¹/₄in (6mm) using the V-tool and No. 8 gouge to remove material before 'bosting' down carefully around the edges and levelling the background with narrow flat chisels.

4 Use a marking gauge to scribe two lines around the sides of the panel, one ³/₈in (10mm) from the back edge, and the other ¹/₄in (6mm) from the back. Now make the outer mouldings of the frame using moulding planes, if you have them, or gouges. Plane a concave moulding down to the ³/₈in (10mm) line. Plane across the short ends first as the grain is inclined to break away at the corners – avoid this by always planing inwards at the corners. When you come to the long sides, make sure you form a clean mitre at the corners. The convex 'ridge' moulding can only be planed halfway over with the moulding plane, as it then meets the downward curve on the inside of the corners. This must be finished cleanly with gouges.

5 Finish the mouldings with a ¹/₈in (3mm) cove around the edges, planing down to the lower of the two lines marked earlier. Take care to get a neat finish on the frame. It can be sanded later, but not yet as the grit may get on the carving and blunt your tools.

7 Now shape the olive leaves and stems. Use a No. 8 gouge to create a central ridge in each leaf. Make sure you cut on the 'downstream' side of the grain in each direction, otherwise you will break bits out. Give the ridge a natural curve to reflect the flow of the pattern, and the leaves a slight tilt and curl with a No. 5 gouge. Reduce the depth of the side stems in relation to their thickness, and create an overlap where stems cross one another.

FINISHING

8 Round over the olives with a ⁵/₁₆in (8mm) No. 8 gouge, always working along the grain. 'Roll' the gouge over the top, and slightly undercut the olive to make it stand out.

9 Note how the end of the branch is sloped downwards and scooped out with a gouge to create the effect of having been torn off the tree. This is a traditional form for most types of stem in carving, so commit it to memory.

10 Tidy up the edges of the leaves and stems to create a sharp shadow and clean up the background surface where necessary (you can use your chisels as scrapers to get a smooth finish). Sand the outer frame to a smooth finish using 120 and 240-grit abrasive, then polish the whole carving with a good wax furniture polish. A small stiff brush is the best tool for getting the first coat of polish into all the crevices. Follow up with two more coats by cloth over the frame and olive pattern and buff them up well, leaving the background slightly duller. Don't forget to polish the back of the board as well so it doesn't warp.

11 Hang the finished panel on your wall in a place where the light will accentuate the pattern with shadow lines.

Victorian Foliage

Project 6

RENAISSANCE OAK PANEL

When the barbarians overran the Roman Empire in the fifth century it seemed like the classical world would disappear forever. It sank into oblivion for a thousand years, barely remembered even where its visible ruins showed above the surface. Then, in the fifteenth and sixteenth centuries, little by little, it started to re-emerge in what became known as the Renaissance (literally, 'rebirth').

The Renaissance started in Italy, appropriately. As people explored the subterranean ruins, they started to adopt the styles of architecture and decoration they found there. Gradually the Gothic of the medieval world was displaced by the order and sophistication of classical decoration, and steadily it spread beyond its native Italy to conquer Europe once again.

It was slow to get going in England due to a little local difficulty. Following the big bust-up between Henry VIII and the Pope, England was not on speaking terms with Italy and anything Italian was treated with suspicion. So the Renaissance crept into England gradually in the sixteenth century through the influence of Flemish craftsmen. But Scotland enjoyed better relations, and when James VI of Scotland became James I of England in 1603, the Renaissance finally got into full swing.

Apart from the obvious columns and capitals, Renaissance design found expression in a particular form which is the subject of this project – the carved panels which decorated doors, chests and

pilasters. Linenfold and strapwork panelling had been a feature of grand houses for many years (see Project 3, page 34) but now it burst into an exuberant display of classical vases sprouting arabesque swirls of foliage, with cherubs and other figures. This endured through the Stuart period in this oaken form, before reinventing itself as moulded plasterwork in the eighteenth-century classical revival. It continued to flourish in Victorian times as one of their many 'revivals', and some truly outstanding Victorian Renaissance carved panels can be seen at Alnwick Castle in Northumberland, northern England.

I have put together this design from a variety of sources, one of which was a Victorian brass fingerplate in my house. It could fit into any period from 1500 to 1900, but I think that it sits best in the early seventeenth century when William Shakespeare was in his prime, so I have fumed the oak to a Jacobean chocolate brown. If you prefer to leave it in its natural state, just leave it to darken naturally over the next 400 years!

1603–1714 Jacobean and Stuart

1603–1714 Jacobean and Stuart

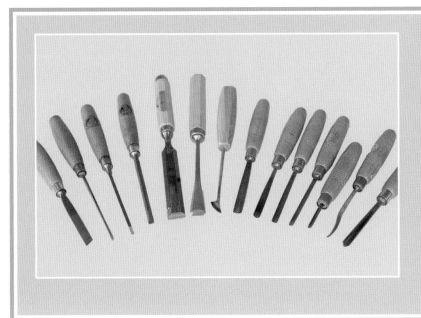

TOOLS AND MATERIALS

Wood: Kiln-dried oak (*quercus robur*), 20 x 10 x 1in (508 x 254 x 25mm)

Tools, *from left to right:* ^{3}/8in (10mm) skew chisel, ^{1}/16in (2mm) chisel, ^{1}/8in (3mm) chisel, ^{1}/4in (6mm) fine-ground flat chisel, ^{3}/4in (20mm) flat chisel, ^{3}/4in (20mm) No. 3 fishtail gouge, ^{5}/8in (16mm) hooked skew chisel, ^{3}/8in (10mm) No. 3 gouge, ^{5}/16in (8mm) No. 8 gouge, ^{1}/4in (6mm) No. 5 gouge, ^{3}/16in (5mm) No. 5 gouge, ^{1}/8in (3mm) No. 5 gouge, ^{3}/16in (5mm) bent chisel, V-tool.

Finishes: Household ammonia (for fuming), good-quality furniture polish if you want a polished finish

GETTING STARTED

1 Prepare a board of planed oak 20 x 10 x 1in (508 x 254 x 25mm). As it will be fumed, make sure it is free from sapwood (the soft white timber on the outside of the tree). Sapwood doesn't respond to fuming and will stay white. Plane the edges and put a slight chamfer on the corners. Trace on the pattern using carbon paper. Normally I would use 'green' oak for carving, but it carries a risk of warping. On a fairly large flat panel like this, warping would be quite noticeable and would spoil the carving, so I have used kiln-dried oak. It is a bit harder to carve (you will need the mallet more), but you can be more confident it will stay flat.

2 Clamp a steel rule along the inner edges of the border and use it to guide a ^{3}/4in (20mm) flat chisel. Cut along the rule to a depth of about ^{1}/16in (2mm) with each cut, then chamfer off the waste on the inner side. Repeat the process a little at a time until you have created a clear straight edge to a depth of about ^{1}/2in (13mm).

GROUNDING OUT

3 Use a No. 8 gouge to remove surplus wood from the 'ground' between the pattern and the border. You will be going to a depth of ¹/₂in (13mm) eventually, but stay just above this depth with the gouge. Carefully work up to the edges of the pattern, using a V-tool in the narrow gaps.

4 With the bulk removed, 'bost' down carefully around the edges of the pattern, and 'ground out' the background with flat chisels to an even depth of ¹/₂in (13mm) all over.

5 To get an even depth, make a simple depth gauge with a screw inserted through a flat piece of wood, set to protrude just under ¹/₂in (13mm). Lay it on the panel and move it all over the ground, then use a chisel to flatten off the patches with scratch marks from the screw until no more appear.

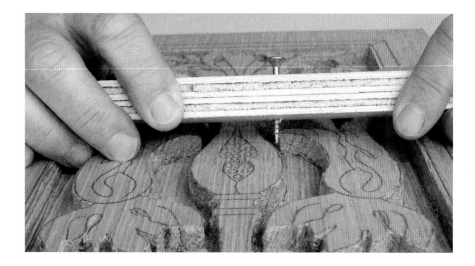

CARVING THE PATTERN

6 The pattern must look as three-dimensional as possible on a flat surface, which is why we have gone to a depth of $\frac{1}{2}$in (13mm). First, shape the base of the vase so its rim is a continuous curve. Shape the 'bulges' on the vase so they appear bigger in the middle and smaller at the edges. This helps to give a three-dimensional effect.

7 The stem and foot of the vase must be shaped to follow the curve of the base, which means lowering the depth in proportion to the width.

8 The open seed pod in the middle of the stem is a common Renaissance feature. To make it look as if the seeds are about to burst out, use a small No. 5 gouge to round over each seed and the point of a skew chisel to clean out the triangles between them. At the base of the pod, make one of the sides lap over the other.

9 Another Renaissance feature is the way the various leaves curve down to the ground along one edge and have a raised edge on the other side, like an escarpment. Use the concave side of a No. 3 gouge to shape the convex curve. Make a clean edge where it joins the ground by careful use of a V-tool.

Renaissance Jacobean

10 Carve the bunches of grapes by rounding over each grape with a small gouge and using the point of a skew chisel to clean up the triangles between them. As with all the features, try to maintain symmetry on opposite sides of the carving.

11 Finish the detail carving with the fan of leaves erupting from the top of the main stem in a flourish.

FINISHING THE BORDER

12 With the detail carving finished we can return to the border. Use the steel-rule trick again to cut a step ¹/₈in (2mm) in from the inner edge and ¹/₈in (2mm) down from the top face. Make it straight and level using flat chisels. Think of this as 'freehand planing' with your hand acting as the plane and the chisel as the blade – it is a good exercise in accuracy.

13 Now use a ³/₈in (10mm) No. 3 gouge to round over the step into a convex moulding running straight and even on all sides. Create a neat mitre in each corner.

FUMING

15 Fuming with ammonia replicates the natural darkening effect of air on the tannins in the oak, but at a rate of about a century an hour. Pour about six tablespoonfuls of household ammonia into a plastic tub large enough to hold this panel (do it in a well-ventilated place, wear eye protection and follow the supplier's safety instructions). Place the panel on some wooden supports to allow the fumes to flow freely around the wood, put the lid on the tub and seal any gaps round the edges.

14 With the border finished the carving is now complete and should look like this. If you want to leave it in its natural 'new' colour just give it a coat of wax furniture polish. But, for an authentic Jacobean look it is time to start fuming.

16 The time it takes to darken depends on several variables (strength and volume of ammonia, temperature, and the volume of your tub), so check the panel every half-hour until it reaches the colour you want. In my case it took about three-and-a-half hours to reach a nice Jacobean chocolate brown. If yours is too slow to darken, add more ammonia and leave it a bit longer.

17 If you fancy a matt finish as I did for this panel, you can just give it a rub over with a dry cloth and leave it unpolished. If you prefer more of a shine, use a good wax furniture polish, such as Antiquax.

Renaissance Jacobean

Project 7
GOTHIC WINDOW

There can be few more fertile fields for carving than the Gothic. In its Medieval and Victorian Revivalist incarnations its distinctive character is defined by carved ornament and delicate tracery. This panel combines the two most significant features of Medieval Gothic – the moulded window mullions and interconnecting curves that form the tracery, and the stylized, often ghoulish, creatures that inhabit it.

Although this panel is designed for domestic display, its origins are ecclesiastical. The top section, which I have fitted into a typical 'pointed' window, is a direct copy from a book that inspired the nineteenth-century Gothic Revival. Pugin's *Gothic Ornament* is a collection of drawings of authentic medieval ornament copied mainly from churches and cathedrals in England and France. It was produced in 1828 by A.C. Pugin – father of the more famous A.W.N. Pugin, shining star of the Victorian Gothic Revival. It is still in print today from Dover Publications and is an excellent source of Gothic detail for woodcarvers.

Carving this panel gives you a chance to practise both architectural features and life forms, of a sort: there are three pairs of part-real, part-fantasy, creatures – dogs, lions and birds – but none of the pairs is identical. One dog has its ears down and the other has them swept back – I don't know if there is any symbolic significance in

this, but that is how Pugin has drawn them. With the birds, their bodies face towards the centre, but they both have their heads facing to the left of the panel – one looking over its shoulder and the other apparently pecking at its foot. Pugin's drawing shows them looking slightly menacing and primeval. The lion heads are more similar, but their manes and ears are slightly different. Assuming that Pugin's drawing is accurate, we will be recreating the creatures exactly as their unknown medieval creator intended them to be portrayed.

These details were copied by Pugin from the oak original in the old St. Michael's Cathedral, Coventry (central England). Although it is not clear what species the birds are, it would be nice to think they are phoenixes, as this carving was destroyed by incendiary bombs in the devastating Coventry air raid of 14 November 1940. By recreating the panel in this project, we will be 'raising them from the ashes'.

SCALE DRAWING OF THE GOTHIC WINDOW PATTERN ON A 1IN (25MM GRID). ENLARGE THE DRAWING TO THE REQUIRED SIZE.

1066-1485 The Medieval Period

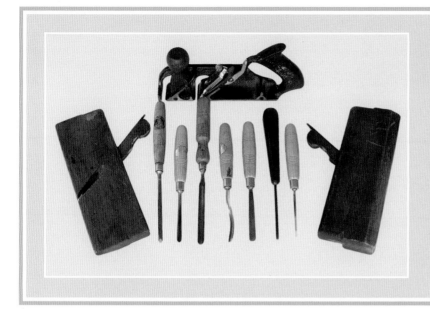

TOOLS AND MATERIALS

Wood: Oak (*quercus robur*),
22 x 17 x 2in (530 x 430 x 50mm)

Tools, *from left to right:* 3/8in (9mm) moulding plane for cove mould, 3/4in (18mm) moulding plane for convex mould, rebate plane, 1/4in (6mm) fine-ground flat chisel, V-tool, 3/8in (10mm) No. 8 gouge, 5/16in (8mm) No. 8 curved gouge, 3/8in (10mm) No.3 gouge, 1/8in (3mm) No. 9 gouge, 1/16in (2mm) veiner.

Finishes: Danish Oil (rubbed on thinly by cloth) or good-quality furniture polish

1 A Gothic carving really demands to be done in oak, so prepare a panel of 'green' oak (*quercus robur*) 22 x 17 x 2in (530 x 430 x 50mm), and trace the pattern onto the panel. Much of the pattern will need to be redrawn as surfaces are cut down, but it helps to have it all drawn in at the start. Go over the sawing lines in red so you don't get lost with the jigsaw.

2 Cut out the internal voids with a jigsaw, making allowance for the lower end of the saw flexing out on the curves. Cut the outside edges with a bandsaw, if you have one, to avoid the flexing problem. With the voids and edges cut out, the boundaries of the pattern are now fixed.

TRACERY

3 Use a marking gauge to create two lines around the outside and inside edges at depths of ⁵/₁₆in (7mm) and ⁵/₈in (15mm) from the top face (the ⁵/₁₆in [7mm] line defines the tracery level).

4 Attach the panel to a backing board, by screwing through from the back, to secure it for carving. Clamp the board to the bench and move it around as required. With a rebate plane (or a chisel) cut a rebate from the edge of what will be the convex moulding down to the ⁵/₁₆in (7mm) line. Replicate the rebate on the internal edges using a flat chisel.

5 With a ³/₄in (19mm) moulding plane for a convex mould, if you have one, or the inside of a No. 5 gouge if you don't, round off the convex ridge surrounding the arch.

6 Using a ³/₈in (10mm) cove-moulding plane if you have one, or a No. 8 gouge if you don't, cut a cove around the outside of the arch from the tracery level down to the ⁵/₈in (15mm) line. The inside edge of the cove should leave a ¹/₁₆in (2mm) shoulder beside the top ridge.

7 Cut the whole surface of the centre mullion (the window bar) down to the tracery level, stopping at the lion heads for the time being. Replicate the cove on the inside edge of the window, including both sides of the centre mullion, using a No. 8 gouge.

8 Reduce all the tracery surfaces down to the tracery level, leaving just the birds, lions and dog heads at their original level for the time being. You will need to draw back in the outlines of the tracery.

9 With the No. 8 gouge, and a shallower No. 3 gouge, continue the cove moulding from the window mullions around the edges of the tracery, cutting in the triangular 'piercing' between the larger and smaller curves.

TIP: KEEPING
A CARVING CLEAN
When you are drawing directly onto the wood, use crayon instead of pencil. Pencil lead tends to get ground into the wood, making the carving look grubby.

Medieval Gothic

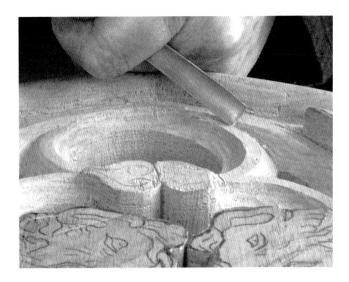

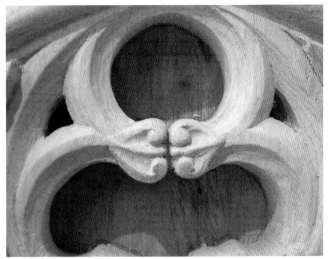

10 The surface of the larger curves (from the lion heads to the peak and sides of the arch) remains at the main tracery level, but the smaller curves (leading to the dog heads and the little 'knuckles' in the middle of the trefoil) are cut down to $^1/_{16}$in (2mm) below this level so that their top surface merges into the coves of the larger curves.

11 Carve the detail on the little scrolled 'knuckles' in the middle of the trefoil.

BIRDS AND BEASTS

DOGS

12 Next, remove the panel from the backing board and turn it over. Cut away the back surface behind the tracery so it ends up about 1in (25mm) thick, leaving the dog and lion heads untouched for now. This will make the tracery stand out from the wall when mounted and will make it look lighter.

13 The project now changes gear as we move from architectural forms to life forms. The tracery stage is finished with the 'creature sections' still at the original level of the board surface. Start the left-hand dog head by cutting the top surface down to $^1/_8$in (3mm) above the level of the tracery curves that the head is joined to. Redraw the pattern with a wax pencil and shape the cove of the tracery into the back of the head behind the ears.

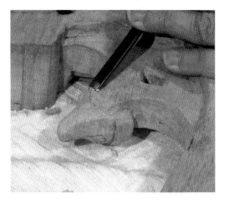

14 Shape the ears into the tracery, form the area behind the eyes, then form the eyes, nose and forehead.

15 Dismount the carving from the backing board and carve away the underside so that the dog's mouth and throat curve into the underside of the tracery.

16 Repeat the process for the right-hand dog, which has its ears swept back.

LIONS

17 The lion heads are left at the original board level. This is so they can lay over the top of the centre mullion where it curves into the tracery. The heads have to look as if they are sloping backwards, so that the tongues loll onto the surface of the mullion and the manes at the back end flop over the large curves, which are at the same level as the mullion. This gives the lions a distinct forehead, eyes and nose that appear to face towards the viewer. Starting with the left-hand lion head, and leaving the face untouched at present, reduce the levels around the face so that the mane slopes back towards the tracery. The ears and side whiskers are at about the level of the tracery, and the tongue (about ^{1}/8in [3mm] thick) is laying on the centre mullion.

18 Mark in the eyes and start to shape the face by cutting a groove across between the nose and eyes, and a smaller groove in the forehead between the eyes. Round the sides and back of the head towards the ears and mane, and shape the nose and mouth. Hollow the ears with a ^{1}/8in (3mm) U-shaped gouge, carefully shape the tongue, then give the mane and side whiskers a 'hair' texture with a fine veiner, parting the ends of the 'hair' with a V-tool. Put in 'eyebrows', and a split in the nose curving to both sides of the mouth, also using the veiner. Repeat the whole process for the right-hand lion head.

19 With the carving of the heads finished, dismount the carving from the backing board and turn it over, as we did for the dogs. Shape the underside of the lion heads into the underside of the tracery.

20 The two finished lion heads are very similar, apart from differences in the mane and ears, all copied exactly from Pugin's drawing of the original.

BIRDS

21 Cut the surface of the bird panels down to ¹/₈in (3mm) above the tracery level, and retrace the pattern. The birds are presented differently from the lions and dogs in that they are in a low-relief triangular panel. Some parts of the bird sit above the level of the tracery, and some are incised below it. Start with the left-hand bird by 'bosting' around the edges of the pattern and chamfering the edges of the tracery into the panel. 'Bost' around the body where it meets the upper wing and the leaf.

22 Carve the detail on the upper wing and the leaf.

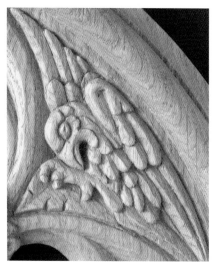

23 Repeat the process on the lower wing. The feathers need to be bold and angular – not soft and feathery – or they will not cast the shadows needed to make them visible from a distance.

24 Complete the lower wing and the foot. Cut a deep hollow under the bird's throat and shape the 'shoulder' so the beak can lay over it. Finish off the body feathers, rounding the body at the edges.

25 When the left-hand bird, with its alert stare is finished, repeat the process for the right-hand bird, which looks rather more sinister with its head down and its 'shoulder' hunched.

FINISHING

26 With all the carving finished, bring up the colour in the wood with a wax polish or a thin coat of Danish oil, rubbed in with a cloth. Mount it on a wall where the light will strike it obliquely to sharpen the shadows.

> **TIP:** CREATING SHADOWS
> With low-relief carving (like the birds on this panel) you need to create shadows to make the detail stand out. Create angular edges, and hang the carving where the light will strike it obliquely.

Project 8

THE PEACOCK OF RIGA

Wandering around the Latvian capital of Riga on a rainy day, I was struck by many beautiful buildings and, in particular, by a large and very striking Art Nouveau peacock design on the front of a grand building declaring itself to have been built in 1902. The panel was beautifully stylized in typical Art Nouveau form, the peacock feathers supplemented by stylized flowers on angular stems emanating from the peacock's beak.

The Riga peacock was a design triumph, except for one thing – the peacock's body. It seemed to have been designed by someone more familiar with chickens, and had been given a fat, ungainly breast and short stumpy wings – all very un-peacock-like and at odds with the elegance of the rest of the design. Although it seemed presumptuous to correct the original designer's work, I felt obliged to restore its dignity. By referring to pictures of real peacocks I have redrawn the body of the bird in a more fitting style without altering the rest of the design.

Art Nouveau literally means 'New Art'. It has close associations with Paris, where the 1900 Exposition Universelle de Paris (Paris World Fair) inspired the likes of Cartier, Lalique and even the Paris Metro to employ this exciting 'new art' to lead the stuffy nineteenth-century world into a new age and a new century.

The heavily stylized plants and flowers of the Art Nouveau style captured the imagination of the young and forward-looking artists and architects of the day and soon spread across the world to become the dominant style of the period. In Eastern Europe it became known by its German name Jugendstil (youth style) and, about this time, Riga was undergoing a period of expansion. What better style for a new and forward-looking city than the very latest look in architecture and decoration, so Riga became one of the great Art Nouveau cities of the world.

Art Nouveau generally suits low-relief carving, so I have used a board only 1in (25mm) thick. Normally I would recommend using green oak as it is easier to carve, but because this is a long, thin panel the risk of warping is quite high, so I used kiln-dried oak. Life is full of compromises, and the extra difficulty of carving dry oak is balanced by the comfort of knowing it is less likely to warp in a heated room.

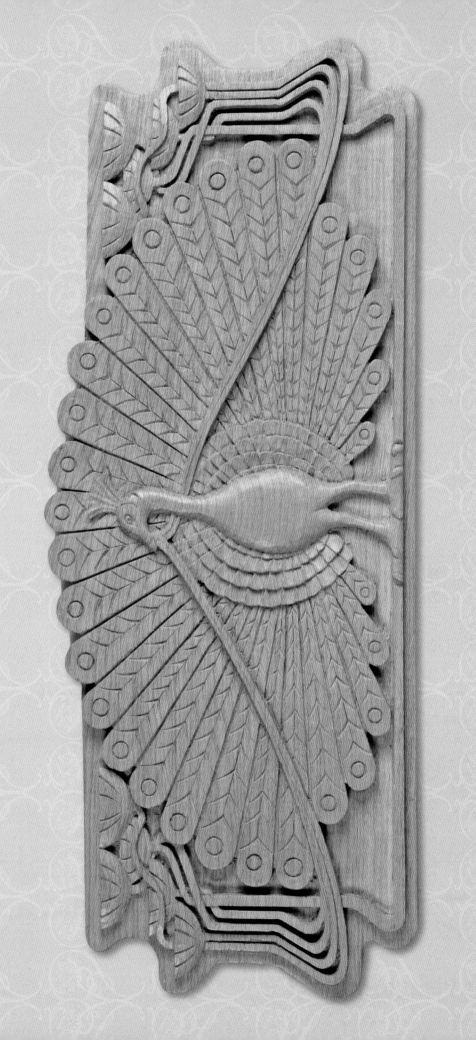

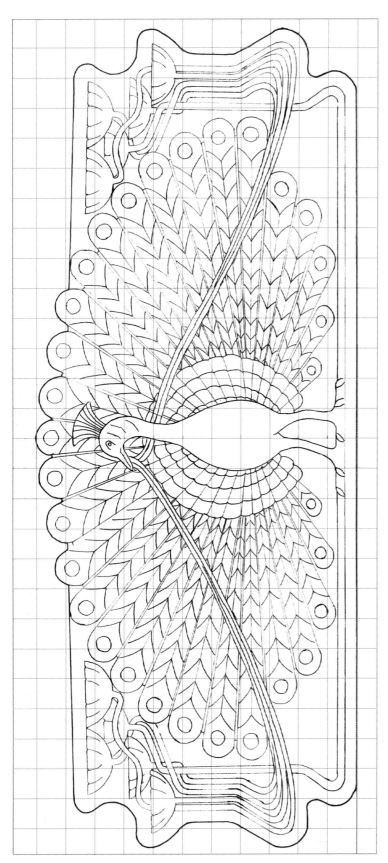

SCALE DRAWING OF THE PEACOCK PATTERN ON A 1IN (25MM) GRID. ENLARGE THE DRAWING TO THE REQUIRED SIZE.

1901–1910 Edwardian

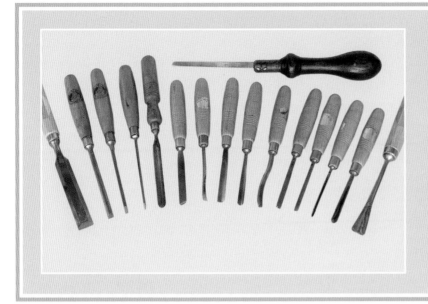

TOOLS AND MATERIALS

Wood: Kiln-dried oak, 28 x 11 x 1in (711 x 279 x 25 mm)

Tools, *from top, then left to right:* padsaw, $3/4$in (20mm) flat chisel, $1/4$in (6mm) fine-ground flat chisel, $1/8$in (3mm) chisel, $1/16$in (2mm) chisel, $3/8$in (10mm) No. 8 gouge, $3/8$in (10mm) skew chisel, $3/16$in (5mm) bent chisel, $3/8$in (10mm) No. 3 gouge, $5/16$in (8mm) No. 8 gouge, $5/16$in (8mm) No. 8 curved gouge, $1/4$in (6mm) No. 5 gouge, $3/16$in (5mm) No. 5 gouge, $1/16$in (2mm) veiner, V-tool, $3/4$in (20mm) No. 3 fishtail gouge

Finish: good-quality furniture polish

PREPARING THE PANEL

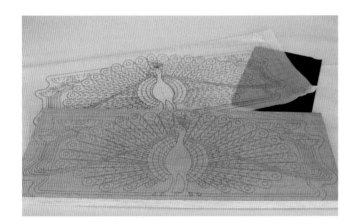

1 Start by tracing the pattern onto a board of oak 28 x 11 x 1in (711 x 279 x 25 mm) with carbon paper. This takes a while as the pattern is very complex. Use a ruler for the straight lines. Try not to miss out any of the pattern.

2 Cut carefully around the edge of the panel with a jigsaw or scroll saw. The panel has a convoluted edge typical of Art Nouveau and some of the bends are quite tight, so use a narrow blade and keep it moving to avoid scorching the wood. The blade will flex out a little on the bends, so allow room for this. Clean up the edges with planes and chisels.

GROUNDING OUT

3 Use a marker gauge to scribe a line around the edge of the panel $^{1}/_{2}$in (13mm) from the face. Use a No. 8 gouge to 'ground out' the background sections, and also the outer border. This will all be cut down to a depth of $^{1}/_{2}$in (13mm), using the marker gauge line for guidance.

4 Finish the grounding-out by paring down the vertical edges of the pattern and smoothing the flat surface of the background. Check the depth of the background with a simple depth gauge, made by fixing a screw through a flat piece of wood with $^{1}/_{2}$in (13mm) protruding.

CARVING THE PEACOCK FEATHERS

5 When I get to this stage in a carving I am always reminded of a phrase workmen often used to use – 'Let the dog see the rabbit'. You don't actually need a dog (or indeed a rabbit) but it is important to get a clear view of the task. When the background is all blocked out and the pattern is standing clear, you can more easily see where to go with carving the detail. The dog can see the rabbit.

6 The main tail feathers must 'dish' inwards, under the long strands coming from the peacock's beak, meeting the inner feathers at a level about $^{3}/_{8}$in (10mm) below the original surface. Use a V-tool to define the edges of the long strands. To define the edge of the inner feathers you need to go a bit deeper – cut down vertically with a No. 3 gouge a little at a time, followed with slanting cuts until you have created a vertical edge initially about $^{1}/_{4}$in (6mm) deep along the line of the inner feathers.

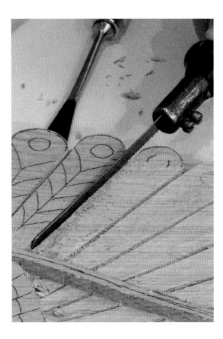

7 One of the problems when you start carving detail is that you effectively erase the drawn pattern as you work. On some carvings this doesn't matter too much, but it does matter here! This is a complex geometrical pattern with lots of straight lines and, if you lose them, it is unlikely you will be able to produce a good result. You need to keep track of those straight lines as you carve down, so use a broad flat chisel to make incisions about 1/8in (3mm) deep along the feather edges, and keep re-cutting them as you work down.

8 Use a broad No. 3 gouge to 'scoop' a shallow hollow along the length of each feather, sloping gradually towards the line of the inner feathers. It will take a few tries to get the level right. Keep re-cutting your straight lines as you work down. Where feathers go under the long strands, make sure the line and level follow through.

9 The narrow gap between each feather is difficult. Get a clean edge with the flat chisel, then clean out the gap with a padsaw.

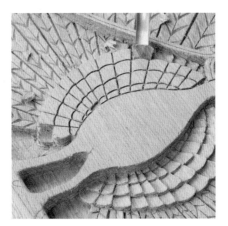

10 Now we mark in the feather detail. Make vertical cuts with a broad No. 3 gouge, followed by angled cuts, to form a 'V' for each curving line. Use the broad flat chisel again to cut a thin straight line down the middle of each feather. Use a No. 5 gouge to cut the circular 'eye' at the outer end of each feather (an important peacock feature).

11 With the outer feathers formed, now work on the inner feathers. Use a No. 3 gouge to form the vertical edges of each ring of feathers, and to scoop out each part. Create a more pronounced 'dishing' effect, with the inner edge about 3/8in (10mm) below the surface of the peacock's body.

12 With all the feathers carved, turn the board over and use a rebate plane to finish off the back of the top feathers. Where they protrude above the top of the main edge of the board, plane away 1/2in (13mm) at the back, so the tops of the feathers are the same thickness as the parts that are on the background.

CARVING THE PEACOCK'S BODY

13 Form the plume on the peacock's head by cutting grooves with a No. 8 or 9 gouge, but take care as you are cutting across the grain. Round over the head and neck with a No. 3 gouge, and shape the ends of the long strands into the peacock's beak. Carve the eye and make a small indentation for the pupil with the tip of a veiner. Cut two grooves at the back of the head to signify the black and white colour markings of a real peacock.

14 Shape the peacock's body so that the flat section in the middle rounds smoothly over into the sides. Carve the legs and feet by sloping the 'knees' backwards towards the background, and shape little toes at the end of the feet. Leave the legs a bit flat at the front to keep the Art Nouveau effect – it is not a wildlife carving and needs to follow the period style.

CARVING THE STEMS AND FLOWERS

15 Now the peacock is finished, turn your attention to the stems and flowers. These are very stylized and really identify this carving as an Art Nouveau design. Start by reducing the level of the strand which runs along the baseline to a depth of about ³/₈in (10mm) above the ground. Shape the strand that goes from the peacock's beak to the outer edges by giving it a smooth flow. Use a V-tool to separate it into two and then three strands as it gets towards the outside. The stems then separate into a spaghetti-like muddle before they reach the flowers, so I used colour-coding with wax crayons to identify which stem belongs to which flower (don't use highlighters or felt tips – they will soak in).

16 'Bost' down carefully a little at a time to open out the gaps between the stems and around the flowers. Take the wider gaps down to the ground level, but only go as deep as you reasonably can in the narrow gaps or you will break bits off. You can now see more clearly where each stem goes.

FINISHING

17 Two of the five flowers are set slightly behind the other three and it helps to carve these first, to get your levels. Work the individual stems to the correct level, so that they pass over and under other stems to reach their own flower. Give the stems a flat surface like a ribbon. Re-cut the narrow gaps between stems as you work down. You can then shape the three forward flowers, rounding them at the sides with a No. 3 gouge. Finally, use the No. 3 gouge to make four cuts in each flower to divide the 'petals'. Keep the Art Nouveau style firmly in mind and do not stray into realism.

18 Art Nouveau tends to look best with a smooth finish, so a little light sanding with fine abrasive is permitted to remove any rough surfaces. A good-quality furniture polish is the best finish. Use a stiff brush for the first coat to get in all the crevices, then another coat by cloth. Don't forget to do the back as well or it might warp.

19 Buff your carving up to a good shine, and hang it on your wall. Much of the detailing is very shallow, so it will show up better if the light strikes it sideways.

Art Nouveau

Project 9

THE DRAGON OF EYE

In the small Suffolk market town of Eye, in England, there lives a dragon. Admittedly he is rather a small dragon, carved in stone and barely 9in (23cm) tall and, though he does not breathe fire or carry off maidens, he looks like he would have your finger off if you went too near him! He resides on a Victorian Gothic monument to a local benefactor who died in 1886, and caught my eye as I was driving through Eye.

Quite by chance, I later discovered a design for this same dragon in a book – *Victorian Foliage Designs*, now published in facsimile by Dover Publications. The designer was James K. Colling (1816–1905), a well-known Gothic Revival architect of the time. He published this book of designs in 1865, pre-dating the Eye monument by at least 21 years. Although the foliage had been adjusted to fit the triangle of a Gothic pediment instead of the original quatrefoil, it is clear that the Eye dragon, and probably the whole monument, was designed by Colling.

Here is my adaptation of the 'Dragon of Eye' as a woodcarving project. I have tried to copy the dragon exactly as it appears on the Eye monument and in Collings' illustration, but I have amended the foliage yet again by increasing the number of leaves and flowers (dove's foot cranesbill according to Collings' notes) to five. This creates a continuous ring of foliage around the dragon which allows us to form a pierced framework of leaves instead of a solid background, giving the carving a lighter and livelier look.

I have used green oak for this project as I think it suits the Gothic Revival style, and for the same reason I have used a simple wax finish. However, any suitable carving wood and finish will do provided they contrast with the wall where you intend to hang the panel.

Dragons are perennially popular with children, and those of a Gothic persuasion, so you will have no difficulty finding a home for this one.

SCALE DRAWING OF THE DRAGON OF EYE PATTERN ON A 1IN (25MM) GRID. ENLARGE THE DRAWING TO THE REQUIRED SIZE.

1837–1901 Victorian

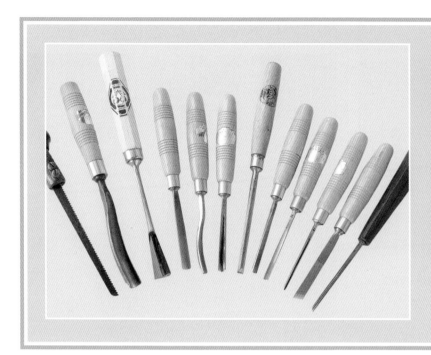

TOOLS AND MATERIALS

Wood: Oak (*quercus robur*),
13 x 13 x 2in (330 x 330 x 51mm)

Tools, *from left to right:* padsaw,
$5/8$in (16mm) No. 9 curved gouge,
$3/4$in (20mm) No. 3 fishtail gouge,
$3/8$in (10mm) No. 3 gouge, $5/16$in (8mm)
No. 8 curved gouge, V-tool, $1/4$in (6mm)
fine-ground flat chisel, $5/16$in (8mm)
No. 8 gouge, $3/16$in (5mm) No. 5 gouge,
$1/16$in (2mm) No. 11 veiner, $3/8$in (10mm)
skew chisel, $1/8$in (3mm) No. 9 gouge.

Finish: good-quality furniture polish

BLOCKING OUT

1 Start by making a full-size copy of the drawing. Take a piece of 'green' oak 13 x 13 x 2in (330 x 330 x 51mm) and some carbon paper. Align the pattern so the grain goes crossways, as this will help with carving the head and wings. Trace the pattern onto the oak, and go over the cutting lines in red so you don't get lost with the jigsaw.

2 Cut out the internal voids first while you still have the outside to clamp to the bench. Drill access holes for the jigsaw then carefully cut out using a blade at least 3in (75mm) long. Remember the bottom end of the jigsaw blade will tend to flex outwards on the curves, so make allowance for this.

Victorian Gothic

ROUGHING OUT LEVELS

3 If you have a bandsaw, use it to cut around the outside of the pattern to avoid the flexing problem. If you don't have a bandsaw, continue with the jigsaw.

4 Attach the panel to a backing board by screwing from the back into the centres of the leaves. One of the main issues you will need to deal with in this carving is establishing the relative levels of all the features of the dragon and foliage without losing track of the pattern as you go. Start by reducing the level of the leaves to 1in (25mm) thickness from the back face. Take care with cross-grain sections of leaf as they will break off if you are too rough with the mallet. Draw the pattern back on afterwards with a wax pencil (graphite pencils make the wood grubby).

TIP: WATCH THE GRAIN

When drawing a carving pattern onto a block of wood, take note of how grain direction will affect the practicalities of carving and the final appearance. Align the grain either vertically or horizontally to follow the strongest lines of the pattern and avoid creating awkward cross-grain weaknesses. In this carving, the dragon's head and wings make a strong case for a horizontal grain direction.

5 Reduce the flowers to a level of ¹/₄in (6mm) above the leaves. Draw the petals and centres back on. These are only provisional levels, so err on the side of caution and don't remove wood you may need later.

6 Use a V-tool to define the edges of the dragon's left leg, right foot, and the point where the upper body curves over the tail. Rough out the level of the lower body from under the left foot, backwards under the right foot, and up to the point where the tail merges into the leaf. The body should be slightly below the level of the leaves as it passes under the right leg, but keep a natural flow with a slight rise as it meets the top leaf. You will need to refine the body shape later, so don't be too fussy at this stage.

CARVING THE HEAD AND WINGS

7 Rough out the levels for the upper part of the dragon's body, starting behind the head and sweeping down and round below the shoulders of the wings, under the nose, and under the left foot to join the lower body. Leave the dragon's head and wings at the full thickness of the board for now. You will need to reduce the stems of the leaves and flowers to nearer the correct level as you go, and also adjust the levels of the legs and feet.

8 Carve the surface detail on the dragon's head. Create a forehead and nose that face slightly forward, as if the dragon is trying to jump out of the background. The right eye, right ear and tip of the nose should be at the top level of the 2in (50mm) thick board, and the left ear should appear to start from the left-hand side of the head. The left eye and the inside of the mouth are formed later.

9 Remove the carving from the backing board and turn it over to undercut behind the head. Use a padsaw to separate the head from where it joins the left side of the body so that there is a gap of about 1/4in (6mm) between the nose and the body. Also use the padsaw to open out the mouth.

10 Now, carefully carve the tiny teeth with a small, fine chisel. Push a small gouge down inside the mouth to hollow the jaw between the teeth. The horizontal grain direction works against us with the tiny teeth (a necessary compromise), so just try to give the impression of teeth.

Victorian Gothic

CARVING THE FOLIAGE

11 Carve the wings with a large No. 9 gouge, sloping them so they appear to come out of each side of the body. To create sharp ridges on the wings, always cut on the 'downstream' side of the ridge. This is where the horizontal grain direction really helps – it would be difficult to create sharp ridges across the grain without some crumbling.

12 Now turn your attention to the foliage again, as it needs to be reduced to its final levels before we can get proper access to all of the dragon's body. Carve the leaves and their stems to give a natural curve and curl. The levels have been left high so far to allow room to put in plenty of rise and fall as you scoop out the leaves with a large gouge. Create ridges down the centre of each leaf, and merge the stems into the dragon's body.

13 Carve the flowers to stand slightly above the leaves. Use a No. 5 gouge to round over the centre, then make two scooping cuts in each petal towards the centre with the same gouge.

14 Detach the carving from the backing board again and place it upside down on a soft surface. Undercut the leaves and flowers to a thickness of about $^1/_4$in (6mm) at the edges, and round off the underside of the dragon's body. Check to make sure it all looks right from the front.

FINISHING THE DRAGON

15 To shape the spine along the dragon's body, start by cutting a line of small circles with a ¹/₈in (3mm) No. 9 gouge. Be careful to follow the curve as illustrated in the pattern as this gives the body a dynamic twist along its length. Use a V-tool to cut a groove about ¹/₈in (3mm) deep along each side of the row of circles, so the circles stand up as a ridge. Reshape the body to remove the grooves.

16 Use the inside of the No. 9 gouge to round over the little spinal knobs, sizing them in proportion to the thickness of the body. Beware of grain direction and keep the work area tidy so that, if a piece breaks off, you can retrieve it and glue it back in place. Use the point of a skew chisel to clean up in between the knobs.

17 Shape both legs and feet with their tiny claws. Create a shoulder where the dragon's right leg joins the body, and make his left leg appear to come from the other side. Make the feet grip realistically on the body and leaf stem, looking as if he is about to pounce!

18 Finish the body by carving a series of convex rib-like scales, following the twist of the body to accentuate the effect of energy.

19 After making any final touches to the undercutting, give the finished carving a good rub over with wax polish and hang it on your wall against a contrasting background, where the light strikes it obliquely.

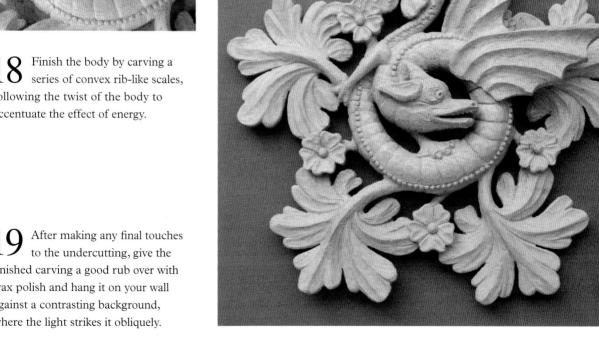

Victorian Gothic

Project 10

ST IVES FOLIAGE PANEL

Design in the later Victorian period was dominated by foliage. It occurred inside and out of their buildings and eventually erupted all over their rooms in the wallpapers and fabrics of William Morris. Much of it is stylized and much is natural. This design falls into the second category. It is, by and large, based on nature. I have not been able to put a precise botanical name to it, but it appears to be a type of bramble (blackberry).

I came across the original panel in St Ives, Cambridgeshire (eastern England), carved in stone in the lobby of a Victorian church. I was struck by the simplicity of the design, which seemed to have a greater impact on the surrounding space than a more complex pattern would have done. In drawing this up into a carving pattern, I made several attempts to expand the design into something more complex, but each alteration seemed to detract from, rather than enhance, the pattern. In the end, I decided to leave it almost unchanged.

I say 'almost' because a design must relate to its setting. To bring out the lightness and delicacy of the foliage in a domestic setting, I felt it should be presented against a contrasting background. The foliage is too thin to stand alone as a pierced carving, so a base panel in a contrasting wood would give it the structural integrity it needs while allowing the foliage to look light and delicate. Lime is an ideal wood for the foliage, with a darker wood for the base panel. I used American walnut because I had a piece the right size, but any dark wood will do. The base panel only needs to be $^5/_8$in (16mm) thick, and I have shaped it to echo the fingerplates that were so popular on doors in Victorian times.

The beauty of using this appliqué method is that it allows the foliage to be carved as a 'pierced' carving. This is much easier than carving in the solid – it fixes the outlines of the pattern so you don't lose them as you carve, and it makes undercutting so much easier. With a pierced carving you can do all your undercutting from the back by turning the carving upside down, which enables you to create very thin edges. The finely carved detail can then be fixed to the contrasting base board to be displayed more effectively.

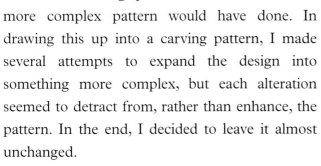

1837–1901 Victorian

SCALE DRAWING OF THE VICTORIAN FOLIAGE PATTERN ON A 1IN (25MM) GRID. ENLARGE
THE DRAWING TO THE REQUIRED SIZE.

1837–1901 Victorian

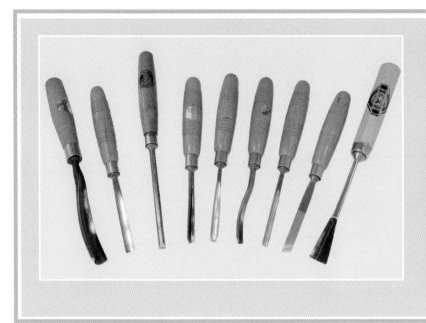

TOOLS AND MATERIALS

Wood: *Foliage:* Lime (*tilia* spp),
15 x 4 x 1^1/$_4$in (381 x 100 x 32mm);
Base board: a piece of a darker wood
such as walnut or sapele, 16 x 4^3/$_4$ x ^{5}/$_8$in
(406 x 120 x 16mm)

Tools, *from left to right:* ^{5}/$_8$in (16mm)
No.9 curved gouge, ^{3}/$_8$in (10mm) No. 3
gouge, ^{1}/$_4$in (6mm) fine-ground flat chisel,
V-tool, ^{5}/$_{16}$in (8mm) No. 8 gouge, ^{5}/$_{16}$in
(8mm) No. 8 curved gouge, ^{1}/$_4$in (6mm)
No. 5 gouge, ^{3}/$_8$in (10mm) skew chisel,
^{3}/$_4$in (20mm) No. 3 fishtail gouge

Finishes: *Base board:* French polish
Foliage: acrylic sander sealer,
good-quality clear wax polish

STARTING BLOCKS

1 Start with a piece of lime 15 x 4 x 1^1/$_4$in (381 x 100 x
32mm), a piece of a darker wood (in this case walnut)
16 x 4^3/$_4$ x ^{5}/$_8$in (406 x 120 x 16mm), and a full-size copy
of the pattern.

MAKING THE BASE PANEL

2 Mark out the base panel with a ^{1}/$_4$in (6mm) cove all the
way around, by drawing a line on the face and sides
^{1}/$_4$in (6mm) from the front outer edge. In each corner, draw
a quarter-circle ^{1}/$_2$in (13mm) in radius, and another ^{3}/$_4$in
(19mm) radius for the cove. This is easier if you cut a right-
angle in a piece of board and push the base panel into the
corner to give you a point to insert the spike of the compasses
into. Draw the ^{1}/$_2$in (13mm) radius on the underside as well,
as this will help later.

Victorian Foliage

3 Use a moulding plane if you have one, or a No. 8 gouge if you don't, to cut a $^1/_4$in (6mm) radius cove across the ends and along each side. It is best to do the ends first, as these are likely to break out at the corners. It helps to clamp a $^1/_2$in (13mm) board alongside the work piece while you are planing or gouging, to keep the cove straight and level.

4 Cut out the quarter circle at each corner with a jigsaw or coping saw, using the $^1/_2$in (13mm) radius line at the back as your guide. Use a No. 8 gouge to carve the cove into the $^3/_4$in (19mm) radial line, and try to get a clean 'mitre' where the coves meet at the corners.

CARVING THE FOLIAGE

5 Sand the board to a good finish, and give it six coats of French polish, applied by cloth. After the first coat has dried, give it a rub over with 600-grit abrasive before continuing with further coats. French polish dries very quickly, so you can apply many coats in a day.

6 Trace the pattern onto the lime block, and cut out the internal voids with a jigsaw. Use a narrow blade on the jigsaw for the tight turns, but remember that it will flex a bit at the lower end, so allow a bit of room for this.

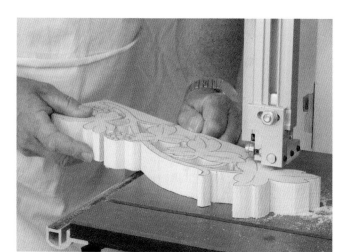

7 Cut around the outside of the pattern with a bandsaw, if you have one, to avoid the flexing problem. If you don't have a bandsaw, continue with the jigsaw.

8 Fix the lime to a backing board of MDF or plywood by screwing through from the back into the leaves at the point where they will be thickest. Mark out the approximate carving levels on the wood using a wax pencil. Marking high points with an 'H' and low points with an 'L' helps when you start carving.

TIP: KEEPING CARVINGS CLEAN
When a lime carving is to be left in its natural finish, it is important to keep the wood clean as you carve. Carving gloves stop the moisture from your hands making the wood grubby, and also protect against cuts and grazes. Use wax pencils whenever you need to draw on the wood, as graphite pencils create a black dust that gets ground in.

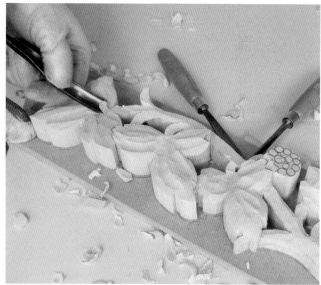

9 Rough out the levels of the stem to give a natural rise and fall that will suit the levels of the leaves and berries where it meets them. There should be at least one point where the underside of the stem will make contact with the base panel after it is undercut later to the same width and thickness. Leave the leaves and berries at their full thickness at this stage.

10 Rough out the leaves with a large gouge, giving them a natural rise, fall, twist and turn. There must be points where the edge comes down close to the base panel. The leaflets will be carved in a convex shape, so lower the levels towards the stem and the outer edges. Consider how each group of three leaflets will lay in relation to each other and their neighbouring leaves, taking account of overlaps.

Victorian Foliage

11 With the levels roughed out, you can carve the berries. They stay more or less at the full thickness of the board. Use a large gouge to round the whole berry cluster into a ball about 1in (25mm) in diameter. Take a ⁵/₁₆in (8mm) No. 8 gouge and press it into the ball, pointing directly towards the centre. Twist the gouge right round to form a circular cut about ¹/₈in (3mm) deep. Repeat the process with another circle beside the first, then another, and so on to form a natural-looking pattern of 'drupes' making up the whole berry. Shape each circle into a hemispherical drupe by taking the same No. 8 gouge and 'rolling' it across the top of the drupe and down into the edge of it in the direction of the grain, then repeat the process in the opposite direction (still with the grain). Clean up the triangular hollows between the drupes with the point of a skew chisel.

12 Next, carve the leaves to their final finish. The best way to give the leaflets a smooth convex shape is to use a large No. 3 gouge upside-down. Curve them down quite sharply into the point where they all meet the stem. Also put a groove along each side (in most cases) with a No. 5 gouge so they have a little 'flip' at the edges. Use a V-tool to carve a groove down the centre of each leaflet into the stem, taking care to get a directional flow that looks natural and lively. Where leaves overlap, think carefully about how the comparative levels will look when you undercut the edges later. The big challenge with the leaves is to create a lively curve, rise and fall and retain the simplicity of the design. Don't be tempted to overwork the carving.

13 Finish the stem by making the vertical and horizontal curves smooth and natural, then carve a shallow cove along the top and sides of the stem and chamfer along the edges. This seems counter intuitive as stems are normally of a circular cross-section, but the stem of a natural bramble is indeed a kind of 'box' cross-section with slightly concave sides, so this is clearly what the original stone carver had in mind.

14 When you are satisfied with the carving of the face, dismount the carving from the backing board and turn it face down on a soft surface. Shave away surplus material from the back to give a sharp edge to the leaves. Away from the leaf edges the wood can be left at a greater thickness and, at the centre of each leaf cluster, there must be an area left at the original base level so it can be glued to the base panel later. Remember to proceed carefully with the undercutting, as the carving is becoming increasingly fragile. Use small, sharp tools as they exert less pressure on the wood than larger tools. Keep the work area clean so that, if any parts break off, you can retrieve them and glue them back in place.

15 When all the carving is finished, give the lime a coat of water-based acrylic sanding-sealer. This will help protect the wood against dirt without changing its natural creamy-white colour. It will also enable you to remove any 'stringy' wood fibres after it dries.

16 Before we glue the lime carving to the base panel, we need to scrape away the French polish at the points where the glue bonds will be. The easiest way to mark these points is to use the pattern tracing, first marking on it the base panel by 'pricking' with a point. Place a dab of suitable wood adhesive on the underside of the lime, then press it onto the base panel in the correct position. Use elastic bands to hold the lime in place and exert a little pressure as it dries.

17 When the glue is set, give the top face of the lime carving a rub over with a clear wax, which will give the surface a slight sheen and protect it without changing its colour.

Victorian Foliage

Project 11

PUGIN COLUMN TABLE

Augustus Welby Northmore Pugin was, without doubt, a genius – a prolific designer of prodigious talent and energy. He was born in 1812, the year of Halley's comet and Napoleon's retreat from Moscow, and he died in 1852, his mind and body broken by self-destructive overwork. He had, as his doctor put it, 'lived 60 years in 40'.

It is largely to Pugin that we owe the Victorian Gothic Revival. He was producing designs for Wyattville's Gothic refurbishment of Windsor Castle at the age of 15. At 23 he was engaged by Charles Barry to produce Gothic designs for the rebuilding of the Houses of Parliament in London. Barry never sufficiently acknowledged Pugin's contribution, but we know that Pugin was responsible for virtually all the interior detail and much of the exterior. In particular, he designed that iconic tourist symbol of London – St Stephen's Tower, known to the world as 'Big Ben'.

Pugin's contribution to the Great Exhibition of 1851 was immense. Its Medieval Court was filled with his High Victorian Gothic designs, manufactured by his long-term collaborators Hardman, Crace, Myers and Minton. It caused a sensation, but at great personal cost – Pugin's health never recovered from the months and years of working day and night, and a year later he died exhausted and tormented.

But Pugin's influence had already spread throughout Britain, and to the world beyond. He was the guiding star that led Victorian Gothic to North America, Australia and Europe. It lives on today in public and private buildings throughout the western world, but most of all in the many new churches built in the nineteenth century.

This turned and carved table is a design I have created using decorative elements from one of Pugin's best-known surviving churches – St Giles in Cheadle, Staffordshire, England. When you enter this church your eyes take a while to adjust to the gloom, but when they do you will be struck by the beauty of its decoration. Gold, red, green and blue emerge from the darkness in spiralling columns of leaves and flowers, multi-coloured chevrons and gilded tracery. This table – one of two projects in this book where a lathe is essential – sets out to capture the spirit of Pugin's authentic Medieval multi-chrome decoration, inspired by the columns and friezes of St Giles.

SCALE DRAWING OF THE PUGIN COLUMN TABLE ON A 1IN (25MM) GRID. ENLARGE THE DRAWING TO THE REQUIRED SIZE.

1837–1901 Victorian

PREPARATIONS

1 Start by making a full-size copy of the drawing – you will need to measure diameters from this with callipers. Prepare two circular 'blanks' of kiln-dried oak 9in (230mm) diameter x 1¹/₂in (38mm) thick, and another two 6in (152mm) diameter x 1¹/₂in (38mm) thick. Prepare a piece of lime at least 4¹/₄in (108mm) square x 16½in (420mm) long – you may need to laminate two pieces together to get the thickness.

TURNING THE COLUMN

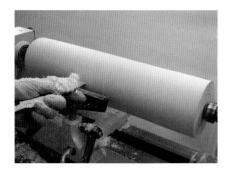

2 Mount the lime block between centres on the lathe, taking care to centre the ends correctly. Turn the block to a cylinder exactly 4in (102mm) in diameter along its whole length, using first a roughing gouge then a straight-edge scraper. Use a steel rule to check it is straight, and use callipers to check the diameter.

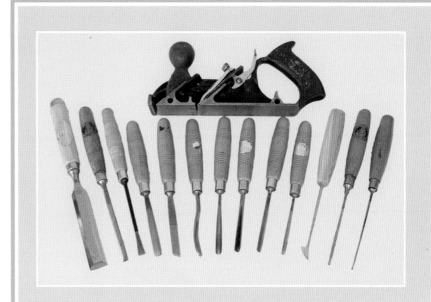

TOOLS AND MATERIALS

Wood: *Table top and base*: Oak (*quercus robur*), two circular 'blanks' 9in (230mm) diameter x 1¹/₂in (38mm) thick, and two 6in (152mm) diameter x 1¹/₂in (38mm) thick. *Column*: Lime (*tilia* spp), 4¹/₄in (108mm) square x 16¹/₂in (420mm) long

Tools: Woodturning lathe (see page 13) and appropriate turning tools (*not illustrated*); *from left to right*: 1¹/₂in (38mm) rebate plane, ³/₄in (20mm) flat chisel, ¹/₄in (6mm) fine-ground flat chisel, ³/₈in (10mm) No. 3 fishtail gouge, ³/₈in (10mm) No. 3 gouge,

³/₈in (10mm) skew chisel, ⁵/₁₆in (8mm) No. 8 curved gouge, ⁵/₁₆in (8mm) No. 8 gouge, V-tool, ¹/₄in (6mm) No. 5 gouge, ³/₁₆in (5mm) No. 5 gouge, ⁵/₈in (16mm) hooked skew chisel, ¹/₈in (3mm) chisel, ¹/₁₆in (2mm) chisel

Finishes: Good-quality furniture polish (table top and base), acrylic paint (sap green, ultramarine blue, crimson red, gold)

Gilding materials: Imitation gold leaf (about 10–12 sheets), gilding size, French polish (as sealer)

3 Mark ¹/₄in (6mm) in from each end to leave a length of exactly 16in (406mm) between the lines. Turn a spigot at each end up to these lines. The spigot forms a tenon which must fit into a mortise in the table top and base. The mortise in these sections needs to fit your chuck in expansion mode, so the diameter of the spigot depends on your chuck. A 2¹/₄in (57mm) spigot suits my 3¹/₈in (80mm) chuck, but you may need it larger for a 4in (100mm) chuck. Square up the ends of the column so it will sit tightly against the top and base.

Victorian Gothic

TURNING THE TABLE TOP

4 Fix a waste block to a faceplate and glue this to the face of the 9in (230mm) diameter blank that will be your table top. Use the tailstock to centre it and compress the joint while it sets. Next day, level off the underside of the blank and glue the 6in (152mm) diameter blank to it. Give it a coat of PVA wood glue on the joining faces, centre and compress it with the tailstock and clamps, and leave it to set.

5 Next day, cut a mortise in the underside of the smaller blank to fit the spigot on the end of the column. Level off the face of the blank and test the fit of the spigot. Work down two beads and a cove on the smaller blank, checking the diameters against the drawing with callipers.

6 On the wider blank, cut a wide cove curving smoothly out to the outer edge, ending about $^1/_2$in (13mm) from the top face. Use a $^3/_8$in (10mm) bead former to create a bead around the outer rim, curving over into the top face. This completes the underside of the table section. Sand it to a fine finish.

7 Dismount the piece from the lathe and remount it on the chuck using the mortise. Check it is centred and balanced so the outer rim runs true when the lathe revolves. Turn away the waste block from the face. Work the bead on the outer rim smoothly round into the table top, cutting down about $^1/_8$in (3mm) into the surface. Smooth the whole face down to this level with a flat scraper and sand it to a fine finish.

8 Polish the top and underside, with the lathe rotating, using a good wax polish (I use Antiquax). Hold the cloth between finger and thumb (do not wrap it around your fingers) so it will snatch out if it gets caught. Use masking tape to ensure that you do not get any wax on the smallest bead at the mortise end, as this will be gilded later.

10 Smooth off the outer rim to a $^1/_2$in (13mm) square edge, and sand and polish as before (remembering to leave the bead nearest the column free of wax). Reverse the base section onto the chuck using the mortise hole. Make sure it is perfectly balanced and centred so the table doesn't end up standing at an angle – the upper and lower faces must be perfectly parallel. Level the bottom, leave a rim of about 1$^1/_4$in (32mm), and cut away the area inside it to a depth of about $^1/_4$in (6mm). This will avoid it rocking on the floor.

TURNING THE TABLE BASE

9 Glue up the large and small blanks for the base in the same way as the top, but without the waste block (screw the faceplate directly to the large blank). Cut the mortise to fit the column and create two beads and a cove on the smaller blank as before. On the wider blank, form a cyma-recta moulding (a concave and convex curve). This is designed to look heavier than the table top to give a better balance – both visual and actual.

FORMING THE SPIRALS

11 Remount the column on the lathe. Mark a point on the circumference at the bottom end. Measure the circumference from this mark with a fabric tape measure, divide it by four, and mark the quarter points around the base. Draw four lines along the column from these quarter points to the top end, checking they are straight and parallel. Now divide the length of the column into six equal portions (about 2$^2/_3$in [68mm]) and draw lines around the circumference at these points turning the lathe by hand.

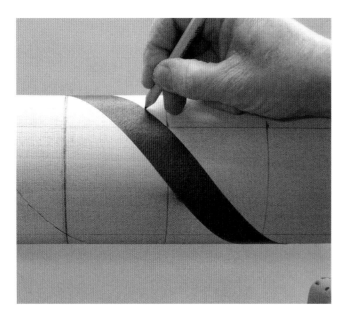

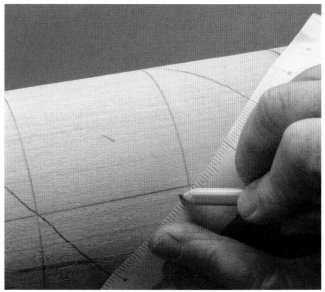

12 Starting from two of the quarter points on opposite sides of the bottom end of the column, 'join the dots' across the diagonals of the 'squares' created by your lengthways and circumference lines. Work from top left to bottom right (with the column horizontal) using masking tape to form your line, and draw a pencil line along its edge. This method is worth remembering as it is the traditional way of marking spirals for 'barley-sugar' twists.

13 When you have marked two spiral lines from the opposite quarter points, you should have a gap of about $4^1/\mathrm{sin}$ (104mm) between them. If our spirals were all going to be the same width we would repeat the process from the other two quarter points, but we are going to have one broad spiral and one narrow one. Measure $2^1/\mathrm{4in}$ (57mm) from the first spiral line (at right-angles to the line) and draw another line parallel to the first to create the broad spiral. This should leave another strip of about $1^7/\mathrm{sin}$ (48mm) for the narrower spiral.

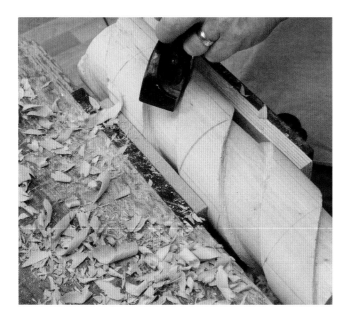

14 Now we need to cut a rebate $^3/\mathrm{sin}$ (10mm) deep along the narrow spiral. Use a tenon saw to cut along the spiral lines to just above this depth (mark the depth on the saw with masking tape), then use a rebate plane to work down to the depth. This is best done in a vice.

15 Use a plane to slightly round over the wider spiral into a 'barrel' profile, with its edges $^1/\mathrm{sin}$ (3mm) above the rebated narrow spiral. We are now ready to start the carving phase.

CARVING THE PATTERN

16 Blow up a copy of the detail pattern to full size, so the 'rose and briar' pattern fits the length and width of the broad spiral. Mark the halfway point on the column and centre it on this. Tape the tracing to the spiral, with some carbon paper under it, and trace the pattern.

17 Cut out the narrow (quatrefoil) spiral strip from the tracing. Because the rebate is $^3/\!_8$in (10mm) below the original surface, it effectively creates a smaller column within the original 4in (100mm) column. This means the pattern drawing, which for convenience is set up for the outer diameter of the column, is too long and wide for the rebated spiral. Simply cut off one of the quatrefoils, and centre the remaining eight along the spiral. Centre the border lines between the edges of the broad spiral, and trace in the quatrefoils and the border.

18 Now, at last, you can start carving the pattern. Use some scrap wood to make a 'cradle' for the column to lay in, with an old towel to cushion it. Use a V-tool and gouges to define the edges of the rose-and-briar pattern. Where it meets the border of the rebated spiral, level the border into the rose and briar so the leaves overlap it slightly.

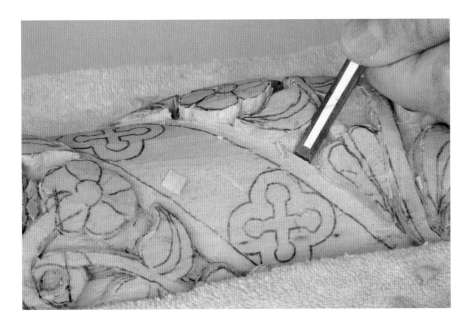

19 Cut a defined edge along the border so that the border strip is about $^5/\!_{16}$in (8mm) wide. Excavate the ground between the stems and leaves to a depth of about $^1/\!_4$in (6mm) so the background follows the same 'barrel' profile as the top surface. The edges of the leaves and stems should be about $^1/\!_8$in (3mm) thick where they overlap the border.

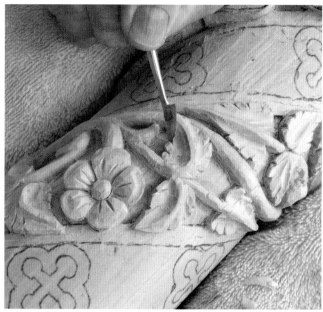

20 Now shape the leaves, stems and flowers to give a natural flow, rise and fall, still retaining the general 'barrel' profile. Use a No. 8 curved gouge to hollow the leaves and create a ridge down the middle.

21 Cut serrations in the edges of the leaves, noting how some of them overlap the stem. Slope the rose petals in towards the centre stamen, and put in small veins pointing towards the centre. Note how some roses are seen from the back.

23 Use abrasives where necessary to smooth the borders and coves, and seal it with sander-sealer. Glue the column to the base and table top – make sure the table stands level, and put some weight on top while the glue sets. When the column table is set, it is ready for decorating.

22 'Bost' a shallow edge around the quatrefoils and hollow out the centre. Use a No. 3 gouge to carve a broad and shallow cove evenly along the spiral between each quatrefoil to give an underlying 'reverse barrel' profile to the spiral. Run the gouge with the grain along each side to get a sharp edge along the border, working gradually towards the middle with a twisting motion that will follow the spiral as you go.

DECORATION

24 Cover the polished oak sections to keep them free of paint. Use acrylic paints to colour in the ground between the pattern elements. The colours I am using (ultramarine blue under the main pattern, crimson red in the cove spiral, and dark green in the quatrefoils) are similar to those used by Pugin in St Giles' Church. When that is dry, paint the raised pattern, quatrefoils and spiral borders with gold acrylic paint or lacquer to give a base for the gilding.

25 Brush a thin coat of gilding size on the areas to be gilded – just one area at a time. The gold leaf will stick exactly where you put the size, so accuracy is essential. When the size is tacky – after about 15 minutes – you can start applying the imitation gold leaf with this simple but effective amateur method (if you want to splash out on real gold leaf, follow the procedure in Project 14). Cut the leaf into pieces about 2in (50mm) square while still in its cover papers. Use a folded piece of paper to pick up a piece of leaf and, slowly and carefully, place it onto the size and press it down with a soft brush. Go over any gaps with more leaf and brush away loose leaf.

26 Imitation gold leaf needs to be sealed against tarnishing. I use French polish (shellac), applied with a brush, as it gives an 'antique' look to imitation gold which otherwise looks too 'brassy'. I used the French polish over the painted areas as well (taking care not to get it on the polished oak) to mute the paint colours and give a more authentic Victorian look. I think Pugin would have approved. Now, with the table finished, you just have to decide whether to put a plant on it or use it as a wine table!

Project 12

FRUIT-AND-FLOWER FESTOON

The fruit-and-flower festoon is one of those Classical forms that has been around since ancient Greek and Roman times. It has its origins in the garlands of real flowers and fruit with which the ancients draped their temples, their heroes and their maidens in times of celebration.

The festoon was soon portrayed in a more permanent form – carved in stone around doors and windows, on vases, pilasters and walls, as with most of their decoration. It took a holiday for a thousand years during the Dark Ages, but returned again in the Renaissance and has never really left us since.

The terminology used for festoons, garlands and swags is not always consistent and is frequently interchanged. Generally speaking, a festoon falls vertically and is often known as a 'drop'. Festoons are often used singly, as this one, or as part of a larger 'garland' surrounding a chimneypiece, door or window. The form reached its zenith in the amazing garlands of Grinling Gibbons (see Project 20).

Festoons were used in all the classically derived styles throughout the seventeenth, eighteenth and nineteenth centuries. I have notionally set this design in the eighteenth century as part of a Georgian decorative scheme, although it is made up from sources spanning three centuries.

The layout of the fruit and flowers in the festoon is based on a Victorian example I saw on a marble fireplace at Alnwick Castle, which is in Northumberland, England – the house manager most kindly gave me permission to photograph it as the basis for this carving. But to give it an earlier feel I added the spiralling ribbon that is commonly found on festoons of the seventeenth and eighteenth centuries. I was inspired by examples at Sudbury Hall, Derbyshire, England, dating from around 1680, and the Peterhof Grand Palace, St. Petersburg, Russia, dating from 1775.

In a grand eighteenth-century house, a festoon would usually be decorated with gilding or be painted white against a pastel background. I decided to go for white, but I felt a solid white paint would be a bit flat, so I compromised and used liming wax to give a more subtle 'antique' whiteness that retained the character of wood – but with a hint of the marble which provided the source for this pattern. (If you fancy gilding it, follow the gilding instructions in Project 13.)

1714–1837 Georgian

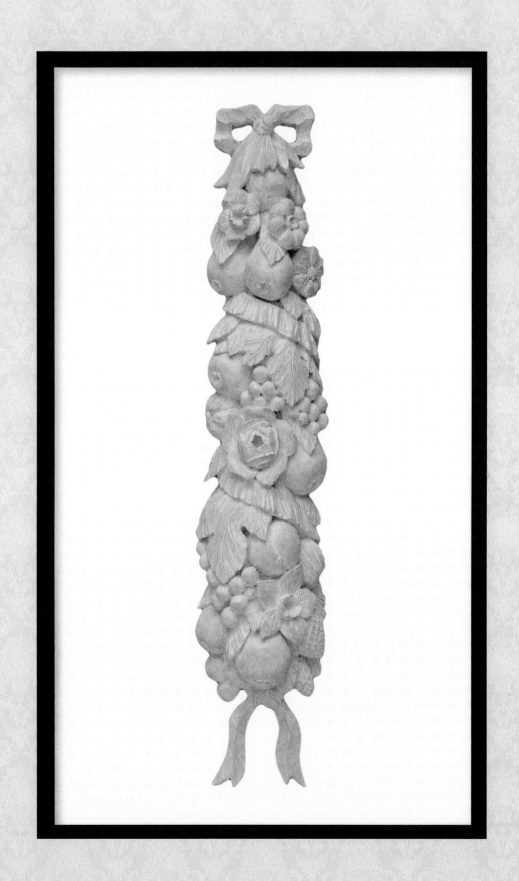

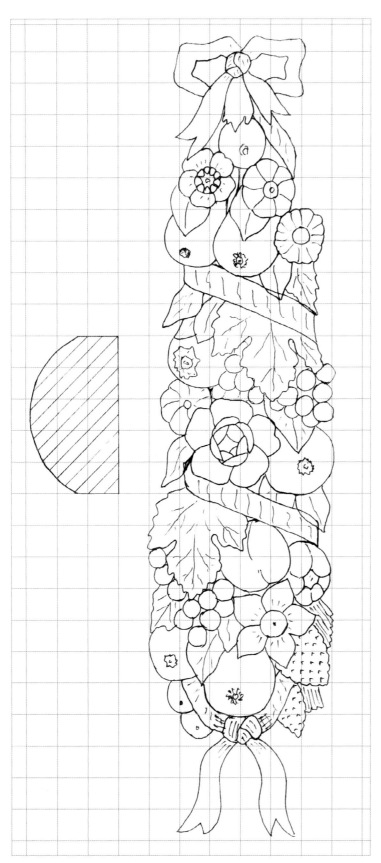

SCALE DRAWING OF THE FRUIT-AND-FLOWER FESTOON ON A 1IN (25MM) GRID. ENLARGE THE DRAWING TO THE REQUIRED SIZE.

1714–1837 Georgian

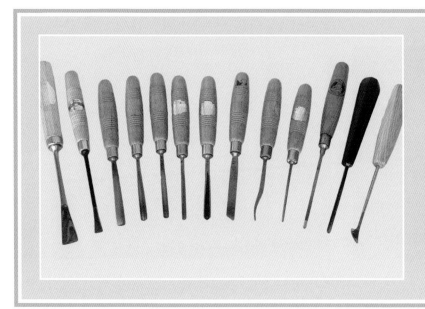

TOOLS AND MATERIALS

Wood: Lime (*tilia* spp), 25½ x 5 x 3in (650 x 125 x 75mm)

Tools, *from left to right:* ³/₄in (20mm) No. 3 fishtail gouge, ³/₈in (10mm) No. 3 fishtail gouge, ³/₈in (10mm) No. 3 gouge, ⁵/₁₆in (8mm) No. 8 gouge, ¹/₄in (6mm) No. 5 gouge, ³/₁₆in (5mm) No. 5 gouge, V-tool, ³/₈in (10mm) skew chisel, ³/₁₆in (5mm) bent chisel, ¹/₁₆in (2mm) No. 11 veiner, ¹/₈in (3mm) chisel, ¹/₈in (3mm) No. 9 gouge, ⁵/₈in (16mm) hooked skew chisel

Finish: Liming wax

STARTING BLOCKS

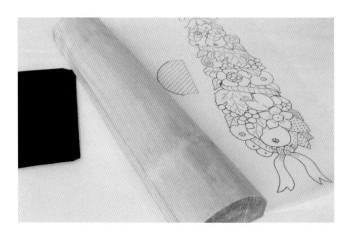

1 Start with a piece of lime 25¹/₂ x 5 x 3in (650 x 125 x 75mm) and a full-size copy of the pattern. If you are sharp-eyed you may notice that the wood is narrower than the pattern. This is because it is a wrap-around pattern that will give us a better three-dimensional base. Draw a line down each side of the block, 1¹/₄in (32mm) from the base at one end, and 1in (25mm) at the other end. Draw a segment of a circle at each end – the 'top' end ¹/₄in (6mm) lower than the 'bottom' end – and plane down the block into this 'barrel' shape.

2 Wrap the pattern over the 'barrel' surface and trace the detail onto the wood using carbon paper.

3 Cut away the surplus wood outside the pattern with a bandsaw (if you have one) or a coping saw.

Classical Georgian

ROUGHING OUT LEVELS

4 Fix the carving to a backing board (screwing from the back) so you can clamp it to the bench, and start working down the levels. Every style of carving has its challenges. With a three-dimensional carving like this, the challenge is in positioning the elements in such a way that they hang naturally around and over one another as though tied together and pulled by gravity. The fruit and flowers should all hang down and outwards when the carving is standing up. When it is laying down with the bottom end towards you, most elements should slope away from you into the background, so it is best to start at the bottom and work your way up. Reduce the level of the ribbons under the pear to about 1¹/₄in (32mm) initially.

5 Continue upwards by rounding off the pears, plums and cones. To shape the pears convincingly it helps if you mark where the 'blossom end' will be, then slope away from this to the top end. Slope the leaves into the background. Working from a traced pattern you will have to fight the tendency to carve too flat. The pattern is only a rough guide to position. To transfer it to three dimensions you need to look at it from the sides as much as the front. You will need to 'bost' some of the side patterns down vertically until they are in the right place, wrapping around the sides and down to the back edge. (Look at the finished photographs to see the relative positions of each element.)

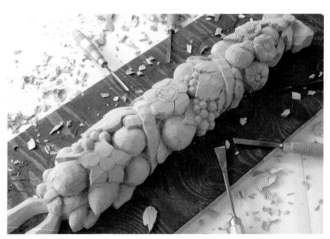

6 Keep moving upwards towards the first spiral ribbon. Refine the lower elements as you establish the positions of the elements above them. You will need to do a little undercutting to get the feel of the depth of the fruit, but wait until you are absolutely sure you have got the modelling right before you go too far. Note how some parts wrap right around to the edge. Add a few extra grapes at the back edge, and extend the grape leaf around the side.

7 By now you will have got the feel of the process, so carry on up to the top. The spiralling ribbons should look as if they are pulling the stalks inwards and holding it all together. Remember what I said about gravity – stand it up and check that everything hangs naturally. When you get to the top ribbon, slope the fruit and leaves back towards the knot so they all appear to be hanging from this point.

1714–1837 Georgian

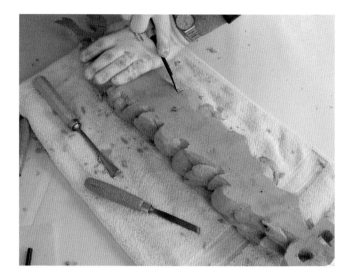

CARVING THE DETAIL

8 To finish the roughing out, dismount the carving from the backing board and place it face down on a soft surface. Undercut the edges so that when you look at the carving from the sides, all the fruit, leaves and flowers wrap around into the underside and seem detached from anything solid. Aim for deep indentations that will prevent the piece looking like a big sausage.

9 Having worked our way up to the top with the rough modelling, we now work our way south again putting in the detail. A prominent feature is the ribbon – use a No. 8 gouge to give it 'crinkly' folds, twists and turns. These contrast with the smoothness of the fruit to give a lively 'crispness' to the carving.

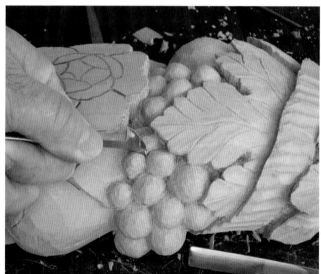

10 A feature common to all the pears and apples is what is known in horticultural terms as the 'blossom end'. It is important to get this in the right place as it determines how the fruit appears to hang. Use a No. 5 gouge to 'prick' a circle in the right spot, create a hollow around the circle, and another one inside it. Shape the bottom of the fruit into the outer hollow, and cut small indentations around the edge to create the blossom remnants you see on real fruit.

11 The grapes and their accompanying vine leaves are defining features of the carving. Use a ³/₈in (10mm) No. 3 or 5 gouge to round over the grapes so each one is separate. Use the point of a skew chisel to clean out the little triangular gaps where they meet. Cut veins in the leaves with a V-tool, giving them a natural flow, and make shallow grooves with a No. 5 gouge in between the veins to give a natural undulating surface. Use the No. 5 gouge again to cut curving indentations in the edges of the leaves, not forgetting the two pronounced 'eyes' separating the lobes.

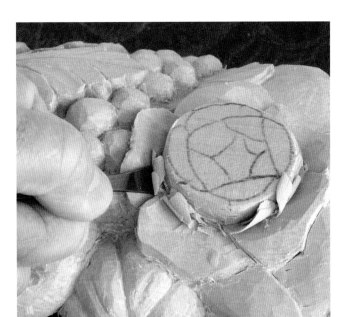

12 There is a technique to carving roses that is worth learning. First, separate the outer petals from the central cluster. Take them down near to the level of the features behind them, otherwise the rose will stick out from the other features with an ugly gap behind it.

13 Next, carve the central cluster of petals so they curl inwards in the middle. Use the point of a skew chisel to cut neat joins and overlaps, and make a hollow in the middle that looks big enough for a bee to climb into.

14 There are three gourds or squashes in this carving which are quite easily carved with a ³/₈in (10mm) No. 3 gouge and a V-tool. There is also a peach in the lower group – make a fairly deep curving groove up the middle and shape the sides into it.

15 As well as the rose, there are several other flowers in the carving. Although each one is different, the principle is the same – carve the outer petals so they curve away from the centre, and make fine grooves with a V-tool or veiner pointing towards the centre.

1714–1837 Georgian

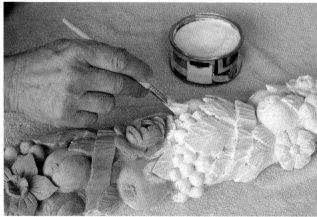

16 Finally, carve the two pine cones by marking out contra-rotating diagonal spirals on the cone surface. Cut a pronounced 'V' along the spiral lines in each direction (a technique worth remembering as it also works for pineapples). The pine needles are simulated by cutting deep grooves with a V-tool and skew chisel.

18 Lime wood varies considerably in colour, and if you are lucky enough to have a piece that is pure creamy-white it may not need any other finish than a coat of wax (see Project 10). My lime is a pinkish light brown, so I decided to go for an 'antique white' effect using liming wax. Brush it on quite thickly and leave it overnight for the wax to set.

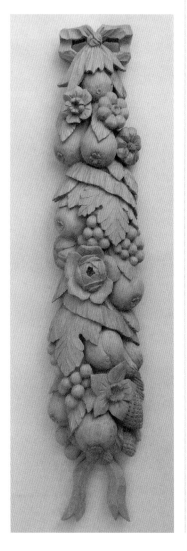

FINISHING

17 Take the carving off the backing board and finish the detailing on features that wrap around to the underside. Undercut the end ribbons to about $^1/_2$in (13mm) thickness. Use 120-grit abrasive to smooth off the parts of the carving that should be smooth (mainly the round fruit). On the more angular parts of the carving, sanding must be kept to a minimum so you don't dull the carving. When you have finished, it should look like this.

LEFT-SIDE VIEW   FRONT VIEW   RIGHT-SIDE VIEW

19 Next day, rub the wood hard with a cloth and a dry brush to polish it to a soft sheen. This will rub away some of the wax to let the wood show through a little on the high spots. It gives the carving a subtle white finish with the character of wood that was last painted 200 years ago and since then has had nothing but the over-zealous attentions of housemaids with dusting cloths. It is the sort of finish you often see in minor stately homes, where later generations living in reduced circumstances have been unable to keep up the ambitious standards of their ancestors.

Classical Georgian

Project 13

ACANTHUS SWIRL

The Baroque style in the late seventeeth and early eighteenth centuries was a very rich period in the history of carving. It took classical forms beyond their hesitant revival in the Renaissance and developed them into an exuberance and richness not seen before, eventually passing the baton onto the wilder Rococo style of the eighteenth century.

The swirling acanthus leaf is the classical form that exceeds all others in abundance. It appears everywhere in classical decoration and in all styles derived from the classical. But the essence of an acanthus swirl carving is not in producing a botanically correct acanthus – it is all about the swirl. Up, down, sideways, in and out – the leaf, the stem, and every part of the carving must be twisting, turning, rising and falling. Curves must be smooth and flowing. A curve that jars will spoil the whole carving – so always keep your mind on the flow of your curves!

This design is derived loosely from a door screen dating from around 1700. I adapted it to suit a gilded wall decoration by giving it more depth, and by creating angular facets on the surfaces to reflect the light when gilded. Gilding is a bit like jewellery – it relies on reflected light. With flat surfaces you just get a gold glow, but give it some angles and it will sparkle like a diamond.

Without gilding, the figure of the wood can distract the eye from the form of the carving. Gilding enhances the form by focusing attention where you want it – on the curves and swirls.

Because this panel is quite a large area to gild, I have used imitation gold leaf (basically brass). It is a fraction of the price of real gold and is easier to use. It is not difficult for a raw beginner to achieve a reasonable 'distressed antique' standard with the methods I will show you. Imitation leaf comes in bigger sheets than real gold leaf, so a pack of 24 leaves will be more than enough for this panel – in fact I only used half a packet.

This carving has a special place in my affections, as it was the first one I made for *Woodcarving* magazine, and was the first step on the road leading to this book. Some of the photos are not as good as later projects, so I hope you will make allowances.

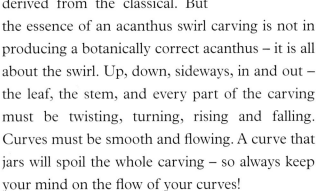

SCALE DRAWING OF THE ACANTHUS SWIRL PATTERN ON A 1IN (25MM) GRID. ENLARGE THE DRAWING TO THE REQUIRED SIZE.

1603–1714 Jacobean and Stuart

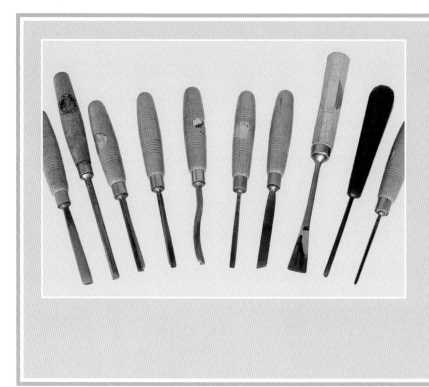

TOOLS AND MATERIALS

Wood: *Main panel:* Lime (*tilia* spp), 16 x 14⁵/₈ x 1¹/₈in (405 x 375 x 28mm) *Flower:* Lime (*tilia* spp), 4¹/₂in diameter by 2¹/₂in deep (114mm x 64mm). Grain direction should be across the diameter.

Tools (*from left to right*): ³/₈in (10mm) No. 3 gouge, ¹/₄in (6mm) fine-ground flat chisel, V-tool, ⁵/₁₆in (8mm) No. 8 gouge, ⁵/₁₆in (8mm) No. 8 curved gouge, ³/₁₆in (5mm) No. 5 gouge, ³/₈in (10mm) skew chisel, ³/₄in (20mm) No. 3 fishtail gouge, ¹/₈in (3mm) No. 9 gouge, ¹/₁₆in (2mm) No.11 veiner

Gilding materials: Danish Oil (as primer/sealer), gold lacquer (as under-coat), at least 12 imitation gold leaves of 5¹/₂in (140mm) square, gilding size, French polish (for sealing and 'antiquing' the artificial gold leaf)

PREPARING THE PANEL

1 Prepare a panel of lime 16 x 14⁵/₈ x 1¹/₈in (405 x 375 x 28 mm). With a board this wide you may need to glue boards side-by-side to make up the width (called laminating). Clamp them tightly together to get a seamless joint, keeping the grain all running the same way. Prepare your pattern and some carbon paper for tracing.

2 With the carbon paper in place and the pattern securely taped to avoid shifting, carefully trace the pattern onto the panel. The board is now a maze of lines, so carefully go over the sawing lines in red and mark the cut-out sections with a cross. This will save you getting lost with the jigsaw.

3 Cut out all the internal voids with a jigsaw.

4 Then cut out the outside edges with a bandsaw, if you have one. If not, continue with the jigsaw.

5 With the voids cut out, the boundaries of the pattern are now fixed. Increase the thickness of the top and bottom edges by 'laminating' with an extra thickness of the same wood. Trace the pattern for these sections onto another piece of the same wood, but with the grain running lengthways along them (at right-angles to the main panel). This will improve strength and give a better grain direction for cutting. Cut out the pieces, glue and clamp them to the main panel.

CARVING THE SWIRLS

6 Next, the carving. Fix the panel to a backing board by screwing through from the back into some of the thickest areas. Clamp the board to the bench with lever-operated clamps so you can move it around easily as you work. 'Bost in' the main edges of the pattern so you don't lose them as you carve down.

7 Remove the bulk of the waste wood with a heavy gouge (or a power carver if you have one) to establish the relative levels of each feature of the panel. Refer to the photos to see which bits are highest and which are lowest when the carving is laying down. Don't take out wood you may need later – it is easier to take more out later than put it back again!

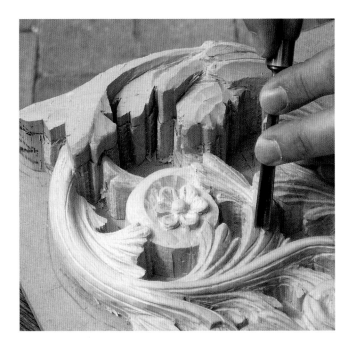

8 Use a V-tool to establish the curves and separate the various features. This is the point where you establish the flow of the curves, so keep checking that your swirls look smooth and natural without any kinks and jerks.

9 Use a No. 3 gouge (convex and concave sides) to shape the smoother faces of the stem and broader leaves.

Gilded Baroque

10 Form the deeper grooves with a small U-shaped No. 9 gouge. This is similar to using the V-tool in the way it establishes the flow of the curves. These U-shaped grooves are the defining features of the surface detail, so try to get them right. Practise on a scrap piece if you need to.

11 Keep checking the flow of your curves to make sure they swirl smoothly around in a 'whirlpool' effect, with the small flower in the centre of the vortex. Use a No. 5 gouge to shape the central stamen of the flower and put the hollows in the petals. Finish the petals with thin 'veins' using a veiner.

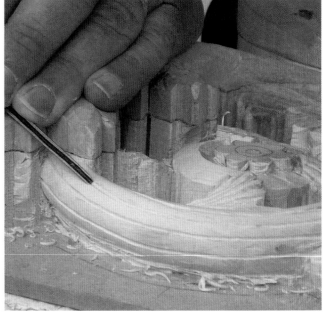

12 Form the stem mainly with the back of the No. 3 gouge, then put in the 'veins' with a fine veiner. Make the veins twist slightly around the stem as they go along it to give a 'sinuous' effect.

13 The thicker part of the stem at the side of the panel needs some undercutting at this stage to round it off with the shallow gouge. Curve the stem up away from the backing board as it nears the raised areas at the corners of the carving. Finish it off with the veiner, twisting around to get the 'sinuous' effect.

14 When the face is finished, remove the carving from the backing board and place it face down on a soft surface. Now, undercut from behind. Pare away the surplus wood with a power carver, sharp chisel or shallow gouge, until the wood is about ⅛in (3mm) at the edges of the leaves. Leave a greater thickness on the parts that are not visible from the front to maintain some strength in the wood.

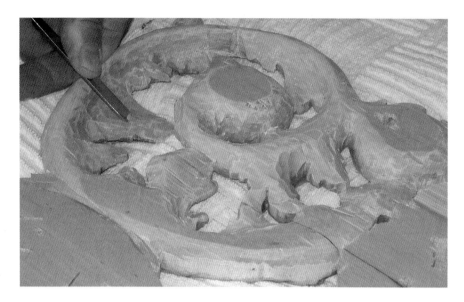

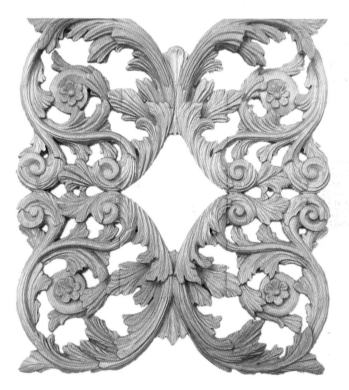

15 The first quarter is now finished. I made one quarter at a time as I was experimenting with the design while the carving was in progress, but there is a lot to be said for working all four quarters together and repeating the same element four times before moving on. That way it is easier to match the features. Each quarter is a mirror image of its neighbours, but you'll be surprised how hard it is to achieve reverse symmetry.

16 As you work the 'reverse symmetry' of the quarters, you will create a horizontal join and a vertical join between each quarter. The lower vertical join ends in a 'spiky' leaf fan – the upper join at the top of the panel ends in an 'unfurled' leaf frond. When all four quarters are complete the main panel is finished. Note that where the panel is given extra thickness by the lamination of the top and bottom edges, the back of the stem is cut away from behind so that, when hung on the wall, it curves away from the wall towards the corners, taking the flatness off the panel and giving it a 'dishing' effect around the central flower.

Gilded Baroque

MAKING THE FLOWER

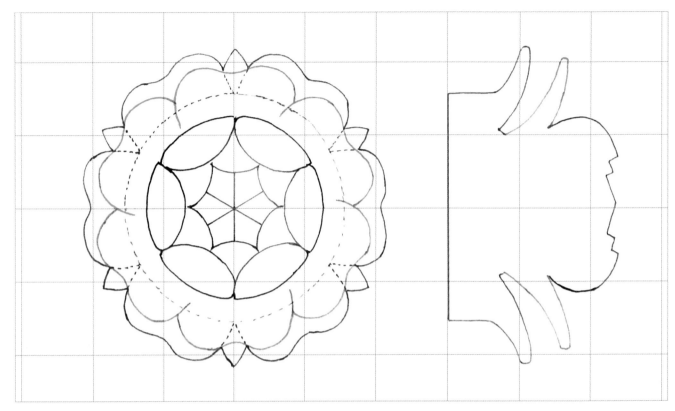

SCALE DRAWING OF CENTRAL FLOWER FOR ACANTHUS SWIRL ON 1IN (25MM) GRID. ENLARGE TO THE REQUIRED SIZE.

17 I have used a woodturning lathe to prepare the flower, as it makes the process quicker and easier. If you don't have a lathe, you can rough out the block with chisels, following the instructions for the lathe. Mount a block of lime on the faceplate of the lathe and turn it to a cylinder of 4^1/$_2$in diameter by 2^1/$_2$in deep (114mm x 64mm). Turn a spigot about 3^1/$_8$in (79mm) diameter x ^{5}/$_8$in (16mm) deep, curving outwards up to 1^1/$_8$in (28mm) from the base. These measurements are approximate as this spigot must fit exactly into the hole in the centre of the panel, and the 'petals' lay over the surrounding carving. Check with callipers and test the fit before proceeding.

18 Using a ^{1}/$_8$in (3mm) parting tool, plunge a cut about ^{3}/$_4$in (19mm) deep towards the centre, and angled towards the base, to form the lower disc of petals. Put a curve on the face. Keep the gap as narrow as your tools will allow. The edge of the disc should be about ^{1}/$_8$in (3mm) thick, getting thicker towards the centre. Round off the rest of the blank into a dome as illustrated.

19 Repeat the process with the parting tool to form the second disc of petals. Plunge in about ³/₄in (19mm) from the edge of the disc so that the internal diameter of the cut is about 2¹/₂in (64mm).

20 Round off the central section of the flower into a dome 2¹/₂in (64mm) in diameter, with its top surface 2¹/₂in (64mm) from the base of the spigot. Undercut slightly as shown, and clean up the face of the top disc of petals.

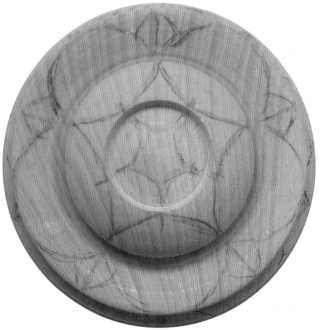

21 Cut a hollow in the top of the dome 1³/₈in (35mm) in diameter, ¹/₈in (3mm) deep at the edge and rising to a point in the centre. Carefully remove the piece from the lathe and test it in the carved panel to check the fit and proportions are correct.

22 Mark up a card into five equal segments, with a 60° angle between each segment. Place the flower in the centre of the card and mark five petals on the lower disc. Divide the upper disc and the centre boss into five petals each, alternating the gaps between the petals on each layer.

Gilded Baroque

24 With a sharp fine chisel, cut around the edges of the petals on the upper and lower discs. Again, shape the joins of the petals to create an overlap. On each petal, carefully make several cuts with a shallow gouge, from the edge towards the centre, to give the petal a natural wavy look. Finish off with a fine veiner, making radial veins in the hollows from the edge to the centre of each petal.

23 With the workpiece held in a vice, carve the central boss of the flower as shown. Where the petals join, cut one edge lower than the other to give the appearance of an overlap.

25 The finished flower should look like this.

26 With the flower glued in position, the carving is finished. If you don't like decorating carvings you could leave it like this (but make sure your lamination joints don't show). If you want the full period look, we'll proceed to a cheap and simple method of gilding that will give us a beautiful 'antique gold' look that will not test your gilding skills too greatly.

GILDING WITH IMITATION GOLD LEAF

27 Give the wood a coat of Danish Oil to seal it, then a coat of a good gold lacquer as undercoat for the gilding. The gold leaf will inevitably split when pushed into the deeper grooves, so the gold lacquer ensures that the gaps are not conspicuous. The job is now ready for gilding. Cut some gold leaf into strips about 1 x 2in (25 x 50mm) while still in its cover papers. Get brushes and size ready. Ensure there are no draughts where you are working – gold leaf will waft away on the slightest breeze. Apply some size thinly to a section of the carving and leave it about 15 minutes to become dry and slightly tacky to the touch.

28 This is a strictly amateur way of applying imitation gold leaf, but it works well for inexperienced gilders. Use the cover papers to pick up a small strip of leaf and carefully place it where you want it. Press it down with a soft brush, then, placing the cover paper over it, press it again with a stiffer brush. Don't worry about small tears or gaps, but go over larger gaps again with more gold leaf. The size will remain active for some time, but if the leaf stops sticking, just apply a fresh coat of size.

29 With the gilding finished, seal it with shellac. Imitation gold leaf can look a bit too bright and brassy if sealed with clear shellac, so I prefer to use French polish, which is just brown shellac. Apply it quickly and thinly, trying not to overlap or you will build up a muddy-looking patch. Try practising on the back first.

30 The finished job. The French polish gives the gold a rich antique glow. It will look very grand hung against a warm dark colour in a place where the light will glitter off the faceted surfaces.

Gilded Baroque

Project 14

ACANTHUS CRESTING

The acanthus cresting dates back to classical times and was a prominent feature of internal and external decoration throughout the seventeenth, eighteenth and nineteenth centuries. It is commonly used on door pediments, at the top of picture frames and mirrors, and above chimneypieces. Its purpose is to lend dignity to whatever is beneath it. It does that very well. It leaves you in no doubt that you should be impressed by the picture, mirror or chimneypiece below it, or by the doorway you are about to pass through.

Crestings take various forms, but most incorporate the classical acanthus swirl to a greater or lesser degree. This cresting is fairly typical of the species, but like most things typical I could not come up with a suitable example from an existing source, so I designed this from scratch as a composite of features commonly found in a cresting.

I have set this example in the middle of the Georgian period. If I had set it earlier or later it would probably have looked heavier and darker. In the Georgian period, decorative carving tended to look lighter and brighter than in the preceding and following periods. This was achieved not only by leaving more 'pierced' space among the pattern, but also by what is known as 'parcel gilding'. In parcel gilding, the word 'parcel' has nothing to do with packaging – it is a corruption of 'partial'.

It refers to the design technique of decorating 'highlights' of the carving with gold leaf. The rest of the carving, in the Georgian period, was normally painted. This combination of gold leaf and paint gave the Georgian drawing room a lightness and delicacy that had not been seen before.

A cresting is almost always symmetrical. If not completely symmetrical in its detail, it has to be symmetrically balanced. That is, the objects on each side of the centre must be the same proportions as their partners on the other side. This design is completely symmetrical, which means we only need draw up a tracing for half the pattern, as we can flip it over to trace a mirror image on the other side. With a symmetrical carving it is generally better to carve the opposite pairs together rather than completing one side at a time, as that way you are more likely to get them both the same.

SCALE DRAWING OF THE ACANTHUS CRESTING PATTERN ON A 1IN (25MM) GRID. ENLARGE THE DRAWING TO THE REQUIRED SIZE.

1714–1837 Georgian Period

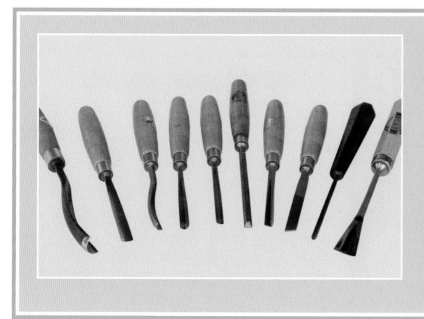

TOOLS AND MATERIALS

Wood: Lime (*tilia* spp),
32 x 9 x 2in (813 x 229 x 50mm)

Tools (*from left to right*): ⅝in (16mm)
No. 9 curved gouge, ⅜in (10mm) No. 3
gouge, ⁵⁄₁₆in (8mm) No. 8 curved gouge,
⁵⁄₁₆in (8mm) No. 8 gouge, ³⁄₁₆in (5mm)
No. 5 gouge, ¼in (6mm) fine-ground
flat chisel, V-tool, 3/8in (10mm) skew
chisel, ⅛in (3mm) No. 9 gouge, ¾in
(20mm) No. 3 fishtail gouge

Finishes: 'Heritage paint' (Farrow
& Ball Dead Flat Oil House White),
acrylic gesso (with red and yellow
food colouring), gilding size,
23¾-carat gold leaf (1 book)

STARTING BLOCKS

1 Start with a piece of lime 32 x 9 x 2in (813 x 229 x 50mm)
and a full-size copy of the pattern. Mark a centre line on
the wood and trace the pattern onto it using carbon paper.
Because the pattern is symmetrical you only need one half
of it, then flip it over to trace the other half using the centre
line to line it up. Mark your cutting lines in red to distinguish
them from the rest of the pattern.

2 Use a jigsaw to cut out the internal voids. Because the
wood is 2in (50mm) thick, the jigsaw blade will flex at
the bottom, so allow some spare room on the bends. It is worth
tracing the pattern on the underside as well (making sure it is
lined up accurately), so you can turn it over to tidy up the cuts.

Classical Georgian

ROUGHING OUT LEVELS

3 Use a bandsaw, if you have one, to cut around the outside. This avoids the flexing problem. Once again, it helps to have the pattern traced on the underside as well – some cuts can only be approached from one direction because of the length of the piece.

4 Fix the wood to a backing board, screwing through from the back. Make sure you put screws into the back of each of the flowers, as these are fragile on their thin 'tendrils'. Because this piece needs quite a complex rise and fall, it is best to rough out all the levels before embarking on detailed carving. Start by reducing the thin tendrils to about $^3/_4$in (19mm) above the base board, and the flowers about $^1/_2$in (13mm) higher.

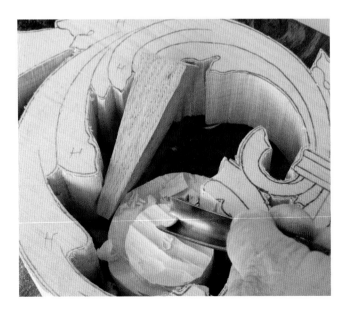

5 As I said, the thin tendrils linking to the flowers are quite fragile – I broke one within five minutes of starting and had to glue it back in place. A good way of preventing this is to use a wedge to give the flower section some support as you rough it out.

6 Rough out the central 'fan' starting about $1^1/_2$in (38mm) above the base board at the top point, going down to about $1^1/_4$in (32mm) in the middle.

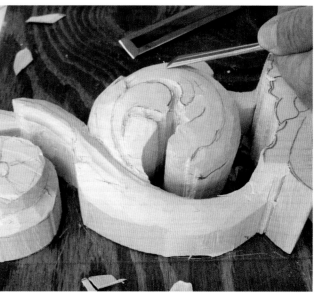

7 Reduce the outer set of leaves down to the level of the outer flower and tendril, with each set of leaves lapping over the other.

8 Just in from the outer leaves is a large curling leaf. This needs to be roughed out into a 'ball', retaining the full 2in (50mm) thickness of the wood at its highest point. Mark the leaf pattern back onto it, but notice how the two-dimensional drawing translates to the three-dimensional leaf ball.

9 Rough out the middle set of leaves so they sprout from the top of the central swirl and curl down to the leaf ball and outer tendrils. Step each set to overlap the other, getting lower towards the outside.

10 Now we are into the important central swirls. This section defines the piece more than any other. The outer edge of the swirl has to be rounded over all the way around. The leaves then need to be separated with a V-tool so they curl round from behind the top of the curve, turning inwards as they progress around the circle. The effect to achieve is like a surfing wave breaking on the shore – keep that image in your mind.

Classical Georgian

DETAIL CARVING

11 With the levels roughed out it is much easier to see how the elements of the pattern relate to one another. Now, start on the detail, beginning with the central 'fan' section. The grain direction is wrong for a simple cut with a V-tool, so the main cuts need to be made from side to side, working with the grain. Make a shallow 'bosting' cut along the edge of each 'leaf', then cut towards it from the centre to the outside to create a shallow 'escarpment' along the edge of each leaf.

12 Carve the detail on the central leaf swirl, using a V-tool to separate the main groups of leaves. Use No. 8, No. 5 and No. 3 gouges to create hollows, twists and turns in each leaf. Make the leaves curl in and down a little towards the centre, keeping a smooth natural-looking flow.

13 Use a small No. 9 gouge to 'drill out' the small 'eyelets' that are a typical feature of acanthus carving. They should appear at the indentations in the leaves so they seem to lap over one another.

14 When you have shaped the upper surface of the leaves, do some rough undercutting so you can see the effect better. Leave enough thickness at the edges at this stage, in case you want to take more off the top. The real undercutting will be done later from the back.

1714–1837 **Georgian Period**

15 When you get to this stage you need to keep checking the appearance of the carving from the angle at which it will be seen, so hang it above head level in your workshop.

16 Continue carving the leaves, swirling outwards to the ends of the carving. Keep the flow smooth and graceful and remember the rule – if the curve is wrong the whole thing looks wrong.

17 To carve the curling leaf 'ball' it is best to cut around the edges of the leaves first, excavating a little into the ball at the edges. Remember this is very three-dimensional and the leaf edges go right round to the back. The whole ball will be hollowed out later, so imagine how it will look when this is done.

18 Now carve all four flowers. Use an ⁵/₁₆in (8mm) No. 8 gouge to round over the centre. 'Bost' in the joins of the petals, and then carve the hollows in the petals with a No. 8 gouge.

19 Finish the surface carving by shaping the 'tendrils' around the flowers and the other tendrils linking some of the leaf groups.

20 Dismount the piece from the backing board for some serious undercutting. Place the carving face down on a soft surface and hollow the leaf balls and the central swirl. Keep checking the appearance from the front as you go. Remember that the flower tendrils are now unsupported and are easily broken off, so go carefully to avoid some emergency gluing!

21 Check the appearance from all angles and, when satisfied, seal the carving with a coat of sander-sealer. It should now look something like this. If you have an aversion to decorating carvings you could leave it as it is but, if you want the full period effect, proceed to the decoration stage.

PAINTING AND GILDING (WITH REAL GOLD LEAF)

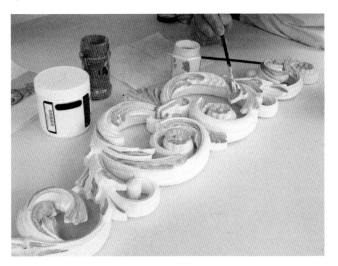

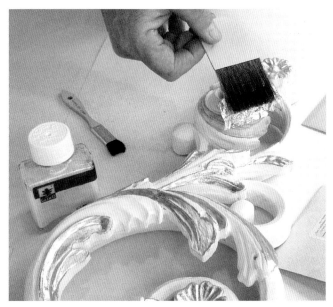

22 By using sander-sealer, a paint primer is not necessary, so go straight to two thin top coats of a suitable 'heritage' paint. To start the gilding process, apply about nine coats of acrylic gesso over the areas to be gilded. To make it easier to see where each coat is going, and to give a background colour to the gold leaf, I added a little red food dye to the first coat of gesso, then yellow in subsequent coats, giving a terracotta background for the gold.

23 Apply a thin coat of size to the areas to be gilded (one section at a time). Remember that the gold leaf will stick exactly where you apply the size, so accuracy is important at the edges. The size will take about 15 minutes to become touch dry. To get the full palatial quality of the Georgian period, I am using real 23³/₄-carat gold leaf, but if you don't want to splash out on this use imitation gold and seal it as in Project 11 (see page 105). Carefully fold back the cover paper on a sheet of gold leaf (it is very delicate) and gently score across the leaf with a knife at the edge of your fold. Cut it into sections slightly larger than the patch you are going to gild. Pick it up with a 'gilder's tip', lower it carefully into position and press it down gently with a soft brush. Brush away loose leaf from the edges and go over bare patches again with small pieces of leaf. Expect to use 20–25 leaves of real gold in total (1 book).

DETAIL OF CENTRE SECTION

TIP: VIEWING ANGLES
When making a carving that will be
placed above head level, hang the
piece in that position frequently during
carving, to check its appearance from
that view.

DETAIL OF OUTER SECTION

24 The gilding brings the whole
piece to life in a way that a
monochrome finish could never do.
Real gold leaf will never tarnish and will
not need a sealer. Mount the finished
piece above a door, a chimneypiece, or
above a picture or mirror frame, and it
will set off the room with a touch of real
Georgian elegance.

THE FULL CARVING

Classical Georgian

Project 15

CHIPPENDALE RIBBON FESTOON

The name 'Chippendale' is synonymous with the very finest of fine furniture –
a name that commands respect and attention in the very best auction houses
on both sides of the Atlantic. Thomas Chippendale (1718–1779) was one of
the greatest cabinetmakers of the eighteenth century, but his talents didn't end
with cabinet-making. He was an outstanding woodcarver and the creator
of what was, in effect, one of the first furniture 'mail-order' catalogues.

T*he Gentleman & Cabinet Maker's Director*, which he published in 1754 (and again in 1755 and 1762), was a book of his designs for chairs, tables, cabinets, pier glasses, girandoles and just about everything a Georgian gentleman or lady may need for furnishing a house. It was, according to his title page, 'Calculated to improve the present Taste, and suited to the Fancy and Circumstances of Persons in all Degrees of Life'.

The pieces were in four main styles – Chinese, Rococo, Gothic, and the newly emerging eighteenth-century version of Neo-Classical. The book was sold as a design source from which gentlemen could order pieces to be made up by Chippendale's workshop, or by any other cabinetmaker of their choice. In his 1762 edition, Chippendale comments that some cabinetmakers claim some pieces (those with the most elaborate carving) are impossible to make – and assures 'all Noblemen, Gentlemen, or others, who will honour me with their Commands' that they can get any design in the book made by 'Their Most Obedient Servant, Thomas Chippendale'. And it is a tribute to his carving skills that this was not an idle boast.

Chippendale's Director, as it is more commonly known, is still available today from Dover Publications. Most things in the *Director* are too large and elaborate for a hobby carving project, but I had for some time wanted to make a carving based on the ribbon motif that appears on several of Chippendale's chair backs. In the current edition there is an extra section illustrating historic examples of pieces in Chippendale style, which includes a photograph of a Rococo 'Carved Girandole' in the Boston Museum of Fine Arts. The upper part of this girandole is just such a ribbon carving. I have adapted the design to create a gilded wall decoration which, although not created by Chippendale himself, is definitely in the spirit of his *Director*.

SCALE DRAWING OF THE CHIPPENDALE RIBBON PATTERN ON A 1IN (25MM) GRID. ENLARGE THE DRAWING TO THE REQUIRED SIZE.

1714–1837 Georgian

STARTING BLOCKS

1 Start with a piece of lime 17 x 6 x 2^1/4in (432 x 152 x 57mm) and a full-size copy of the pattern. Trace the pattern onto the wood using carbon paper. Mark your cutting lines in red to distinguish them from the rest of the pattern, and mark the internal voids with red crosses so you don't get lost when cutting them out.

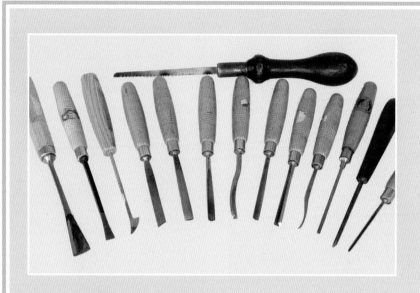

TOOLS AND MATERIALS

Wood: Lime (*tilia* spp), 17 x 6 x 2^1/4in (432 x 152 x 7mm)

Tools (*top, then left to right*)**:** padsaw, ^{3}/4in (20mm) No. 3 fishtail gouge, ^{3}/8in (10mm) No. 3 fishtail gouge, ^{5}/8in (16mm) hooked skew chisel, ^{3}/8in (10mm) skew chisel, ^{3}/8in (10mm) No. 3 gouge, ^{5}/16in (8mm) No. 8 gouge, ^{5}/16in (8mm) No. 8 curved gouge, ^{3}/16in (5mm)

No. 5 gouge, V-tool, ^{3}/16in (5mm) bent chisel, ^{1}/8in (3mm) chisel, ^{1}/8in (3mm) No. 9 gouge, ^{1}/16in (2mm) No. 11 veiner

Gilding materials: Danish Oil (as primer/sealer), gold lacquer (as undercoat), at least 12 imitation gold leaves, 5^1/2in (140mm) square, gilding size, French polish (to seal and 'antique' the imitation gold leaf)

2 Use a jigsaw to cut out the internal voids. On wood this thick the jigsaw is being pushed to its limits, and flexing of the blade is a real problem. It is worth tracing the pattern on the underside as well (making sure it is reversed and lined up accurately), so you can turn it over to tidy up the cuts from underneath. Use a blade at least 3^1/2in (90mm) long, avoid tight turns, and don't cut too near the cutting lines – the blade can flex by as much as ^{1}/4in (6mm) at the bottom. Use a bandsaw, if you have one, to cut around the outside. This avoids the flexing problem.

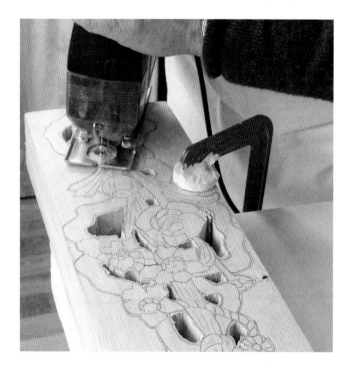

Rococo

ROUGHING OUT LEVELS

3 Fix the wood to a backing board, screwing through from the back. Make sure you put the screws into the thickest parts of the carving, such as the knots and larger flowers. Mark out the relative levels, particularly of the ribbons.

4 Start by roughing out the top ribbon bow. Reduce the ribbons to about $1^1/_2$in (38mm) above the backing board at the high points and $^3/_4$in (19mm) at the low points. Use this opportunity to practise getting a rise and fall in the ribbon, but don't go down to the final surface yet.

DETAIL CARVING – FLOWERS AND LEAVES

5 Continue, reducing the rest of the ribbons (including the central one) down to these levels, taking notice of how they rise and fall into the overlaps and knots. Leave the remaining features at their original level for now, but pay particular attention to how they will affect the level of the ribbons when they are carved later.

6 With the ribbon levels roughed out, start the detail carving by focusing on the pair of acanthus leaves and poppy-seed head in the upper part of the carving. These begin at the full thickness of the board and slope down towards the ribbon knot at the top of the carving. First rough out the slope, then place the carving upright and check it from the front and sides to make sure it has the right flow.

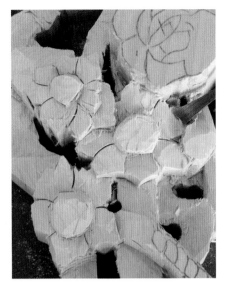

7 Carve the detail on the acanthus using a ⁵/₁₆in (8mm) No. 8 curved gouge to form the main grooves. Switch to a ¹/₈in (3mm) No. 9 gouge as the grooves get narrower, and use a V-tool to part the leaves at the wider end. Shape the poppy head with a No. 3 gouge, put grooves in the sides and stem with a veiner, and cut sharp grooves into the circular head with the V-tool.

8 Move on to the three flowers in the centre of the carving, below the rose. They all face slightly downwards and either left or right. The levels have to be reduced to fit the level of the ribbons. So you don't lose the pattern, it is best to 'bost' down gently until you get to the level. Stand the carving up and check the levels from both sides.

9 Now shape the petals and leaves to give the necessary overlaps. Hollow out the centre 'bowl', and get the appearance as near to a natural flower as you can. Use the veiner for making thin grooves in the petals, all pointing towards the centre of the flower.

10 The large rose must face slightly right and down. First form the centre into a sort of 'ball' with the outer petals curving away from it.

11 Next, shape the individual petals, curling around a hollowed centre. A ⁵/₈in (16mm) hooked skew chisel, if you have one, is a very useful tool for creating sharp creases between the petals.

Rococo

DETAIL CARVING – RIBBONS

13 Carve the surface and sides of the ribbons so they are mostly about ⁵/₈in (16mm) wide and about ¹/₂in (13mm) in depth. Make them rise and fall above the background, and give them a 'crinkly' look with a ⁵/₁₆in (8mm) No. 8 gouge – a typical feature of Chippendale's ribbon chair backs. Parts of the face of the ribbon must come within ¹/₂in (13mm) of the backing board, so their underside will rest against the wall when hung up later. Use a veiner and V-tool to give the impression of 'tightness' in the knots and along the straighter ribbon down the centre.

12 Continue the detailing on the lower portion of the carving. There are two smaller flowers, plus a rope-like twisting stem and a small acanthus-leaf 'tassel'. These are nearer to the backing board, so work the ribbon levels around them.

UNDERCUTTING

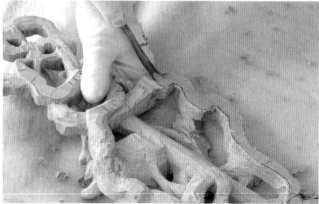

15 Dismount the carving from the backing board and place it face down on a soft surface, such as non-slip matting. Gently carve away surplus wood from the underside of the ribbons, leaves and flowers. Some parts (such as the long thin acanthus leaf) are quite delicate, so use small tools as they exert less pressure on the wood. Curved gouges and skew chisels give more control when you are working one-handed. Protect your hands with carving gloves. Undercutting must be done patiently and will take several hours – don't rush it.

14 Excavate around and under the leaves and flowers to expose the parts of the ribbons that flow underneath them. A padsaw is useful for opening out the gaps. Fishtail gouges are best for carving where access is difficult.

16 Check the appearance from the front and sides, and generally tidy up the carving. You could just hang it on the wall like this but, for a true Rococo feel, it should be gilded. Give the wood a coat of Danish Oil to seal it. When dry, you can 'de-nib' any stray fibres from the wood using fine sandpaper, but keep sanding to a minimum or you will take the life out of the carving.

GILDING WITH IMITATION GOLD LEAF

17 Real gold leaf is expensive, so I have stuck to imitation leaf using the same method as the Acanthus Swirl Panel (Project 13). Apply a coat of a good gold lacquer as undercoat for the gilding. The gold leaf will inevitably split when pushed into the deeper grooves, so the gold lacquer ensures the gaps are not conspicuous. When dry, the job is ready for gilding.

18 Apply some size thinly to a section of the carving and leave it about 15 minutes to become touch dry. Cut some gold leaf into pieces about 1in (25mm) square while still in its cover papers (this is a strictly amateur method, but it works well for inexperienced gilders). Use a folded piece of paper to pick up a small piece of leaf and carefully place it where you want it (lay it over the ridges and curl it into the hollows). Press it down with a soft brush, and brush away loose leaf at the edges. Don't worry about small tears or gaps, but go over larger gaps again with more gold leaf. The size will remain active for some time, but if the leaf stops sticking, apply some more size.

19 Now, seal the gilding. Imitation gold leaf can look a bit bright and brassy, so I prefer to 'antique' it using French polish (brown shellac) as sealer. Apply it quickly and thinly – do not let it run, or you will get muddy-looking streaks (try practising on the back). It will go a bit dull at first, but will brighten up as it dries. Next day, give it a light rub over with a dry cloth, and hang it on your wall. The French polish gives the gold a rich antique glow. It will look very grand hung against a warm dark colour in a place where the light will glitter off the faceted surfaces.

Rococo

Project 16
ROCOCO MIRROR FRAME

When a new town is built from scratch it tends to be designed in the dominant style of its period – bad luck for those built in the 1960s, but good luck for eighteenth-century new towns. When Czar Peter the Great decided Russia should become more European, he built the new imperial city of St Petersburg on the Baltic Sea. The building of its palaces, in the early eighteenth century, coincided with rococo, one of the most exuberant and ornate styles of decoration ever to hit the Western world.

Rococo is the 'wild child' of the eighteenth-century styles. Also known as Louis XV style in its French incarnation, it has the exuberant swirls of the Baroque and the gilded magnificence of Classicism, but with a drunken abandon that often descends into chaos. Order and symmetry are almost non-existent, replaced by wild flowing swirls and almost shell-like curls.

This design is from a series of carved and gilded roundels gracing the ballroom of the Peterhof Grand Palace, outside St Petersburg. This breathtakingly magnificent room was designed by Italian architect Bartolomeo Rastrelli for the Empress Elizabeth in 1751. I chose a circular design because you can make the frame fit any size of circular mirror (I used a 12in/30cm mirror) by making it bigger or smaller without changing the proportions.

The only part of this design possessing any order or symmetry is the circle the mirror fits into. The rest is an almost random arrangement of foliage held together with the aforementioned shell-like curls and swirls. It gives a nod and a wink to the Classical style with the eagle's wing at the top and the ring of circular 'eyelets' around the centre, but chaos seeps in as the circular eyelets morph into ovals before being pulled completely out of shape as though being dragged by gravity.

World War Two was unkind to the Peterhof, when Leningrad (as St Petersburg was called in the Communist era) was besieged by the Nazis. One of their first acts was to burn the Peterhof, and it is a credit to the Russians that they have restored the palace to its former imperial glory – something you can emulate by using this design for your mirror.

1714–1837 Georgian

SCALE DRAWING OF THE ROCOCO MIRROR FRAME ON A 1IN GRID. CROSS-SECTION OF MIRROR FRAME IN THE CENTRE. ENLARGE THE DRAWING TO THE REQUIRED SIZE.

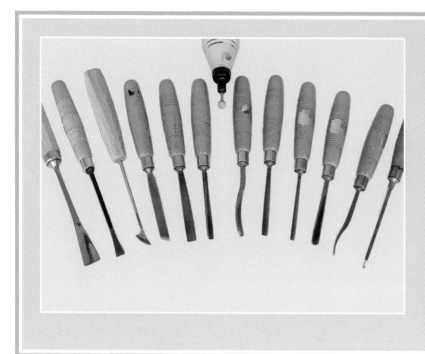

TOOLS AND MATERIALS

Wood: Lime (*tilia* spp),
20 x 22 x $1^3/4$in (508 x 559 x 45mm)

Tools (*from left to right*):
$^3/4$in (20mm) No. 3 fishtail gouge,
$^3/8$in (10mm) No. 3 fishtail gouge,
$^5/8$in (16mm) hooked skew chisel, $^3/8$in
(10mm) skew chisel, $^3/8$in (10mm) No. 3
gouge, $^5/16$in (8mm) No. 8 gouge, rotary
tool with $^3/8$in (10mm) round burr, $^5/16$in
(8mm) No. 8 curved gouge, $^1/4$in (6mm)
No. 5 gouge, $^3/16$in (5mm) No. 5 gouge,
V-tool, $^3/16$in (5mm) bent chisel, $^3/16$in
(5mm) chisel

Gilding materials: Acrylic gesso, acrylic
gold lacquer (as undercoat), water-based
gilding size, $23^3/4$-carat double gold leaf
(about 60 leaves)

MAKING THE FRAME

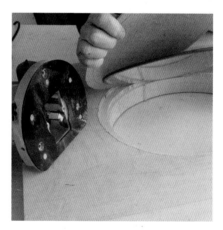

1 First buy your mirror (in this case 12in/30cm) then enlarge the drawing so the circular frame overlaps the edges of the mirror by about $^1/4$in (6mm). Make up a panel of lime to the required size – in this case 20 x 22 x $1^3/4$in (508 x 559 x 45mm). You may need to laminate boards to make up the width. Mark the circle on the panel, using the tracing. If you do this before gluing (using clamps to hold it firm), you can cut out the circle on the bandsaw. Some parts of the carving extend inside the circle, so don't cut them off.

2 With the panel glued together, trace the whole pattern onto it. Use a spokeshave to clean up the inner edges of the frame to get a perfect circle with smooth sides.

3 Mark a line around the inside of the frame about $^5/8$in (16mm) from the back, and use a router (or chisel) to cut out a rebate wide enough for your mirror to fit into. Cut out a shallower and wider rebate behind it for a $^1/8$in (3mm) backing panel.

Rococo

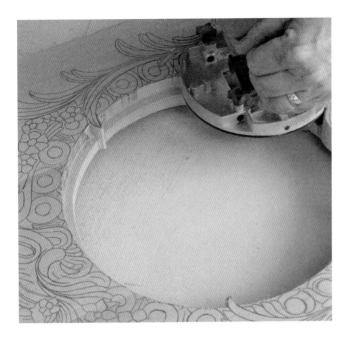

ROUGHING OUT LEVELS

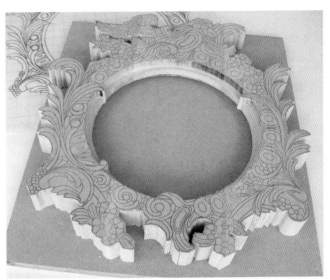

4 From the front of the frame, use a router (or chisel) to cut a rebate about ³/₄in (19mm) deep to form the circular 'mirror ring'. Leave the ring about ¹/₂in (13mm) thick for now. Take the rebate to the edge of the mirror ring where it meets the pattern, and be careful to cut around the elements of the carving that extend inside the ring.

5 With the mirror ring formed, cut around the outside of the pattern with a bandsaw or jigsaw and fix the panel to a backing board, so you can clamp it to the bench.

6 Rough out the level of the 'inner circle'. Take the surface down about ³/₈in (10mm) and round it over to form a circular ridge around the centre. Prick in the outline of the 'eyelets' as you work down so you can keep track of their position to redraw the pattern. Use a No. 3 gouge and skew chisel to shape the mirror ring so it slopes inwards at an angle of about 30 degrees to give a ³/₈in (10mm) thick edge.

7 Moving to the bottom corners, rough out the levels for the wave-like swirls that flow into the palm fronds. Rough out the flowers and leaves that flow from these, finishing about ⁵/₈in (16mm) from the backing board at the lowest points. Prick in the outlines as you go, so you don't completely lose the pattern, then redraw the detail.

PUTTING IN THE DETAIL

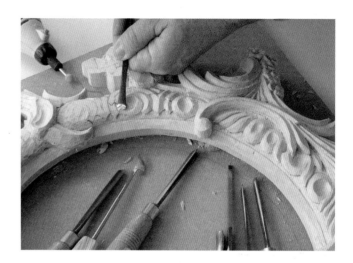

8 The long curving 'palm fronds' are at the highest level of the panel. Slope them towards the outer edges, making sure to get a smooth flow to the curves. Use a V-tool to separate each leaf, and gouges to put a convex curve on one side of each leaf and a concave curve on the other side. These leaves are one of the most noticeable features of the carving, so it is important to get them right. Where they overlap the mirror rim, slope them downwards a little and undercut them into the rim.

9 Carve the detail of the 'inner ring' by hollowing the circles and ovals with a No.8 curved gouge (a rotary burr tool is useful to get a smooth finish in the hollows). Use No. 3 and No. 5 gouges to shape the 'darts' surrounding the hollows. This is basically a wild rococo variation on the classical 'egg-and-dart' moulding.

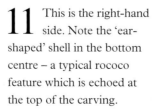

10 Carve the detail on the curls, flowers and leaves. Angle the flowers so they overlap each other in a natural fashion. Hollow out the large curl in the corner to get an effect like a breaking wave. This is the left-hand side.

11 This is the right-hand side. Note the 'ear-shaped' shell in the bottom centre – a typical rococo feature which is echoed at the top of the carving.

ROCOCO

THE TOP SECTION

12 Start the top section by roughing out the flowers and swirls on the left-hand side, moving gradually across to the right-hand side. Pay particular attention to the flow of the curl that extends from beside the central 'ear' shape to the flowers on the outer left edge. In the top right quadrant there is a complex arrangement of swirling fronds – rough out these to get a feel for the levels.

13 The eagle's wing is a typical classical feature, given a slightly wilder look in its rococo form. Rough it out by hollowing the middle and lower parts, leaving the top edge curling over like a breaking wave. The right-hand end of the wing is joined to the rest by a fairly narrow section across the grain, which gives it a potential weakness. Proceed carefully, and if it breaks glue it back together with a support piece at the back running at right-angles to the grain. Rough out the feathers with a V-tool before detailing.

UNDERCUTTING AND SANDING

14 When you are satisfied with the levels, carve in the detail. Here is the top section finished. To the right of the 'ear' there are two small areas that are pierced right through. Try to make a good job of the large daffodil-like flower at the top, sloping it backwards and giving it a small inner ring of petals.

15 With the carving finished, dismount it from the backing board and undercut the edges from behind. Remember the inherent grain weakness in the eagle's wing, so proceed carefully and leave as much thickness as possible behind this section. Undercut the leaves and flowers so their edges are about $^3/_8$in (10mm) thick, leaving a greater thickness away from the edges where it is not visible from the front and sides.

GILDING WITH REAL GOLD LEAF

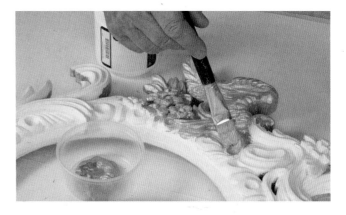

16 The carving is now finished. Seal it with sander-sealer and use fine abrasive where necessary to get a smooth finish on the mirror rim, the long palm fronds and the larger curls and swirls. Keep sanding to a minimum on the flowers so you don't dull the carving. Test the fit of the mirror to correct any shrinkage before decorating.

17 If you want to go for the full palatial finish, as I have done, you will need about 60 leaves of 23³/₄-carat gold leaf (this is expensive, so if you prefer to use imitation gold leaf, follow the process on page 143). For real gold leaf, give the carving about eight coats of acrylic gesso to get a smooth surface for the gilding. You can add red and yellow food colouring to the gesso as I did in Project 14 or, as I did in this case, give it a final coat of gold acrylic paint. The gold leaf will inevitably split when pushed into the deeper grooves, so the gold paint ensures the gaps are not conspicuous. When dry, the job is ready for gilding.

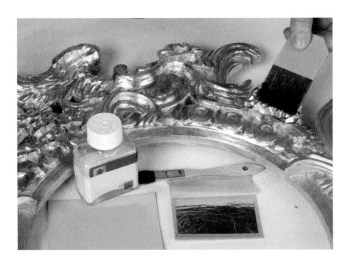

18 Thinly apply gilding size to a section of the carving and leave it about 15 minutes to become tacky. Cut a sheet of gold leaf into pieces about 1¹/₂in (38mm) square with a knife. Use a 'gilder's tip' brush to pick up the leaf (rub the brush in your hair to build up static, then pick up the leaf slowly and carefully by laying the brush against it). Take each small piece of leaf and carefully place it where you want it (lay it over the ridges and curl it into the hollows). Press it down with a soft brush, and brush away loose leaf at the edges. Don't worry about small tears or gaps, but go over larger gaps again with more gold leaf. The size will remain active for some time, but if the leaf stops sticking, apply some more size.

19 With genuine gold leaf the carving needs no sealer. It will stay bright and will never tarnish, needing only the occasional light dusting with a soft brush. It will look very grand hung in a place where the light will glitter off its curves and swirls, and will amply repay the cost of using real gold.

Project 17

GEORGIAN CORBEL

The Georgian period (1714–1837) was the pinnacle of elegance. The Georgian neo-classical room was set out with the perfect proportions of a Greek or Roman temple, and the 'supporting cast' of that scheme of decoration was the gilded corbel. Around the ceiling cornices, under mantelpieces, supporting busts and vases (as here), and whenever something needed holding up, the corbel would be employed.

A corbel is an 'architectural' form that originally projected outwards from a wall to support a beam. It was refined by the ancient Greeks and Romans into the familiar S-shaped volute with an acanthus decoration. In the eighteenth century, the house of a 'person of quality' would not be complete without its classical columns and corbels. In *The Gentleman & Cabinet-Maker's Director* (1754) Thomas Chippendale devotes a whole page to drawing a volute (spiral scroll), like this one, using compasses centred on no fewer than 18 separate foci. I have to admit I am less disciplined – I draw my volutes by eye and tidy them up using French curves!

These days it is unusual to paint a carving, but in Georgian times it was normal for 'architectural' carving to be painted. To keep to the Georgian spirit I painted this corbel with a 'heritage' matt oil paint which, combined with 'parcel gilding' of the volute, the acanthus and the waterleaf detail, gives

the corbel an authentic eighteenth century look. The gilding is also based on traditional methods, though with some concession to the conveniences of modern materials. Gold leaf was normally applied over several coats of gesso which had to be warmed in a pan and mixed thoroughly. Today we have ready-mixed acrylic gesso, which can be used cold straight from the tub it comes in.

Genuine gold leaf, applied over gesso, gives a luxurious finish worthy of a Palladian mansion. This project takes around 40 leaves of genuine leaf ($23^3/_4$-carat). Pure gold is immune to corrosion so it needs no varnish or shellac. It appears quite bright to modern eyes used to seeing Georgian decoration through 200 years of patina, but I have resisted the temptation to 'antique' it. I thought it fitting that it should look as new as it would have looked to an eighteenth-century 'person of quality' adorning their residence in 'the latest fashion'.

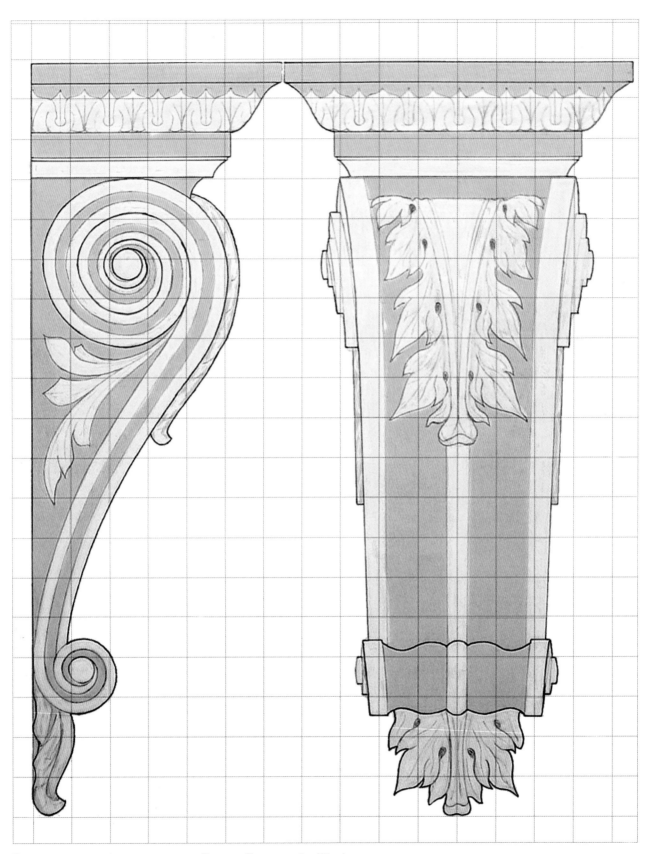

SCALE DRAWING OF THE MAIN PATTERN FOR THE GEORGIAN CORBEL ON A 1IN (25MM) GRID. ENLARGE THE DRAWING TO THE REQUIRED SIZE. SEE ALSO DETAIL PATTERN FOR ACANTHUS AND WATERLEAF ON FACING PAGE.

1714–1837 Georgian

SCALE DRAWING OF ACANTHUS AND WATERLEAF DETAIL ON A 1IN (25MM) GRID. THE CURVED SURFACES MEAN THE ACANTHUS PATTERN ON THE FRONT IS LONGER THAN IT APPEARS ON THE FLAT 'BODY' DRAWING, AND LIKEWISE THE WATERLEAF FRIEZE ON THE ENTABLATURE IS DEEPER. THESE ARE SET OUT FOR TRACING IN THEIR CORRECT PROPORTIONS IN THIS DETAIL PATTERN USING THE SAME 1IN (25MM) GRID. ENLARGE THE DRAWING TO THE REQUIRED SIZE .

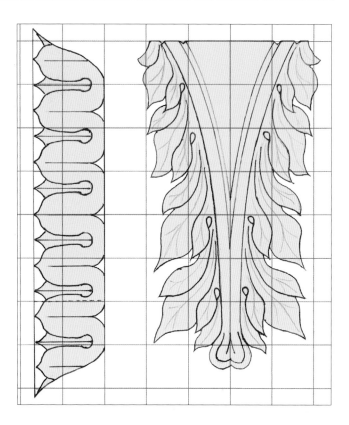

STARTING BLOCKS

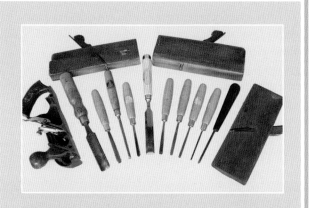

TOOLS AND MATERIALS

Wood: Lime (*tilia* spp): 'body' section block 22 x 6 x 3⅝in (550 x 150 x 90cm) cut diagonally and glued together; entablature block 9¼ x 6¾ x 3in (235 x 171 x 76mm)

Planes: 1½in (38mm) rebate plane, 1in (25mm) convex moulding plane, 1in (25mm) concave moulding plane, ½in (13mm) concave moulding plane. (Concave/convex refers to the moulding – not the plane.)

Chisels and gouges (*from left to right*):
1in (25mm) No. 6 gouge, ⅜in (10mm) No. 3 gouge, ¼in (6mm) fine-ground flat chisel, V-tool, ¾in (20mm) flat chisel, ⁵⁄₁₆in (8mm) No. 8 gouge, ¼in (6mm) No. 5 gouge, ³⁄₁₆in (5mm) No. 5 gouge, ¹⁄₁₆in (2mm) No. 11 veiner, ⅛in (3mm) No. 9 gouge

Adhesive: PVA Wood Adhesive

Finishes: 'Heritage' paint (see step 21), acrylic gesso (+ red and yellow food colouring), gilding size, 23¾ carat gold leaf (about 40 leaves)

1 A block of lime (*tilia* spp) 9¼ x 6¾ x 3in (235 x 171 x 76mm) is needed for the top entablature section. Another block 22 x 6 x 3⅝in (550 x 150 x 90mm) will provide two body sections which can be cut out on the bandsaw and glued (laminated) to form a main body 7¼in (184mm) wide. Trace the side pattern twice onto the 'body' block, with the ends reversed and overlapped. Cut out the two profiles, give both the joining faces a complete covering of glue, then clamp them firmly together until set.

Classical Georgian

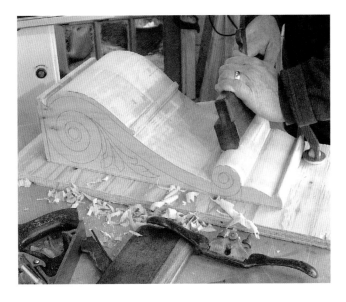

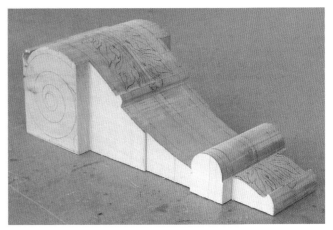

2 Plane the body crossways (use moulding planes if you have them) to the profile set by the tracing lines. The front acanthus section is ¹/₄in (6mm) above the face at this point for carving later (the flip-up at the end will be the 'tendril'). Leave about ¹/₂in (13mm) of spare wood at the top of the body to protect it from damage until we are ready to join the entablature later. Screw the corbel to a board for clamping to the bench.

3 After planing, draw the guide lines back on, and trace on the front acanthus pattern using the detail pattern, which is the correct length for the curve. Cut off the waste wood at the sides with the bandsaw. Leave the scroll sections at the width of their widest point, and a ¹/₈in (3mm) raised area for the side acanthus leaf. Draw the side pattern back on.

CARVING THE VOLUTE

4 After cutting around the edge of the acanthus pattern with a V-tool, cut away the surplus at the sides with a flat chisel to the surface level of the scrolls. Once again, the guide lines need to be drawn back on.

5 Cut away the surplus wood at the back of the scrolls, cut around the leaf pattern with a V-tool, reduce the raised area on the volute down to the proper surface level, then reduce the area around the leaves to ¹/₈in (3mm) below the level of the volute.

6 Form the volute by gradually working down the level in a spiral from the centre boss to the side of the main body, using a broad flat chisel. Clamp the edge of the backing board in a vice when working on the sides.

7 With a $^5/_{16}$in (8mm) No. 8 gouge, cut a groove (or flute) along the middle of the spiral. The flute should be one-third of the width of the volute. Take care to get the edges and bottom crisp and smooth.

CARVING THE FRONT

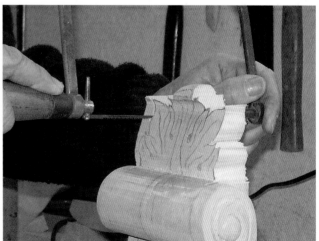

8 Part the leaves on the side acanthus pattern with a V-tool. Use the $^5/_{16}$in (8mm) No. 8 gouge and the back of a $^3/_8$in (10mm) No. 3 gouge to shape the leaves. Make sure you create smooth curves that seem to flow out of the volute.

9 Start the bottom acanthus-leaf section by cutting around the pattern with a coping saw.

Classical Georgian

10 Shape the rounded 'tendril' at the end, then separate the leaves with a V-tool. Use the ⁵/₁₆in (8mm) No. 8 gouge to cut curving grooves in the leaves, lowering the level towards the edges as you go.

11 Take the corbel off the backing board and shave away the edges from the back so the edge of each leaf is about ¹/₄in (6mm) thick.

12 Shape the lower face and the 'bobbin' into a double convex and concave curve. A heavy 1in (25mm) No. 6 gouge is the best tool for the concave curve. The convex curve is tricky as the slope of the face makes it difficult to use the back of a gouge. Scraping with a skew chisel is quite effective, but you will probably need a bit of work with abrasives to get a smooth finish.

13 Start the front acanthus panel by using a ¹/₈in (3mm) No. 9 gouge to cut the 'eyes' in the loops of the leaves, then use a V-tool to separate each group of leaves. Cut the lines in the large 'V' section in the centre with the V-tool, and 'bost' around the edge of the pattern to separate it from the volute.

14 Shape the 'tendril' at the lower end, then shape each group of leaves using mainly the V-tool and the No. 8 gouge. Create smooth curves sweeping down and outwards from the 'eyes' – the appearance of this section will depend very much on the flow of the curves. Use the No. 8 gouge to cut indents in the edges of the leaves to give them a slightly 'spiky' appearance.

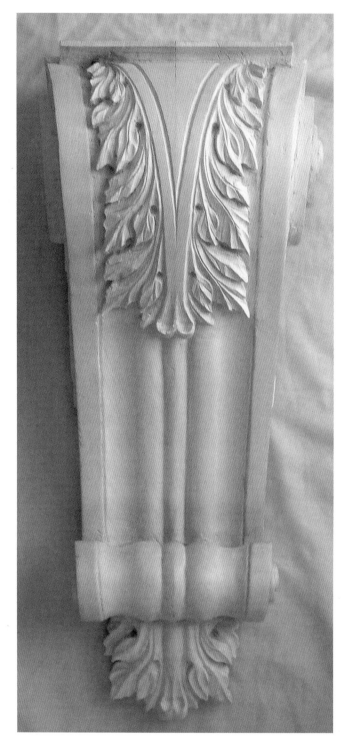

MAKING THE 'ENTABLATURE'

16 Start the entablature by forming the mouldings around the sides. I used traditional moulding planes, but if you don't have any you can form the mouldings with a router or careful use of gouges. You can save some time and work by removing the bulk of the waste wood on the bandsaw, with the table set at a 35-degree tilt.

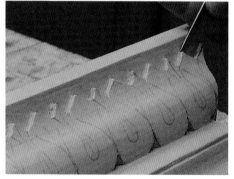

15 With the carving of the acanthus panel completed, and the spare wood at the top of the corbel cut away to its final dimensions, the 'body' section is now complete. Make sure you get an accurate square cut where the body will join the entablature section.

17 Trace the waterleaf pattern onto the wide cyma-recta moulding, using the detail pattern. Make shallow 'bosting' cuts around the edge of the waterleaf, and extend the moulding in between the leaf points. The edges of the leaves should be only ¹/₈in (3mm) thick. At the bottom of the waterleaf, cut a V between each leaf and shape the flat surface into it.

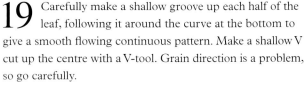

19 Carefully make a shallow groove up each half of the leaf, following it around the curve at the bottom to give a smooth flowing continuous pattern. Make a shallow V cut up the centre with a V-tool. Grain direction is a problem, so go carefully.

18 Use a small gouge to cut the 'eye' in the join of each leaf, twisting it gently around then chamfering from the centre to the edges. Separate the join between the leaves with a V-tool (if the grain allows) or a sharp flat chisel, then chamfer from the centre line to the edges to give a pointed 'spear' with an inverted-V cross-section.

20 The entablature must now be glued to the body and compressed to give a strong bond. The corbel is too big to fit in the vice lengthways, so I improvised with this car jack. Check everything stays lined up properly while it sets.

21 The carving and assembly is now finished. If you have an aversion to decorating carvings you could leave it like this – but if you are ready for the 'full Georgian', give it a coat of sealer (I use Danish Oil) then two coats of a suitable 'heritage' paint (I used Farrow & Ball Dead Flat Oil House White). Paint very thinly over the carving so you don't fill the detail with paint.

'PARCEL' (OR PARTIAL) GILDING WITH REAL GOLD

22 First, apply acrylic gesso over the areas to be gilded to build up a smooth surface for the gold leaf. You will need about six coats on the smooth surfaces of the volute, and nine coats on the carved surfaces of the acanthus and waterleaf detail. To make it easier to see where each coat is going, and to give a background colour to the gold leaf, add a little red food dye to the first coat of gesso, then yellow in subsequent coats, giving a terracotta background for the gold.

23 Apply a thin coat of size to the areas to be gilded, one section at a time. The gold will stick exactly where you put the size, so accuracy is important at the edges. The size takes about 15 minutes to become touch dry. Carefully fold back the cover paper on a sheet of gold leaf (it is very delicate) and gently score across the leaf with a knife at the edge of your fold. Cut it into sections slightly larger than the patch you are going to gild. Pick it up with a 'gilder's tip', lower it carefully into position and press it down gently with a soft brush. Brush away loose leaf from the edges and go over bare patches again with small pieces of leaf.

24 With the gilding finished, the piece comes to life. If you use genuine gold leaf, it will not need sealing and will retain its brightness for very many years.

Classical Georgian

Project 18

DOLPHIN TAZZA

*Dolphins have had a special place in our ornamental vocabulary since ancient times,
and especially so in the Rococo and Louis XV styles of the eighteenth century.
They had a particular significance in France where, from the fourteenth to the eighteenth
centuries, the heir to the French throne was officially titled Le Dauphin (The Dolphin).*

Ornamental dolphins were very rarely portrayed as the mammals we know and love today. To our predecessors, dolphins were fish. They were usually portrayed with scales, spiky fins and even gills. I have kept to this tradition with this design where they are employed holding up the shell dish of a tazza – a bowl on a stem. They are gilded to contrast with the sapele mahogany of the tazza, in the spirit of a period when people delighted in gilded ornament.

For this project you will need a lathe. As hobbies, woodcarving and woodturning have rather become separate disciplines, each going their own way, but in a traditional production workshop there would have been little separation. In the process of 'shaping wood' the lathe would have been just another tool in the woodcarver's armoury, and that is how I have used it in this project. The shaping of the base and stem of the tazza is done entirely on the lathe. The shell dish is initially turned on the lathe into a bowl shape,

and then carved by hand into a shell. The dolphin section is rather more complex. You may wonder how (or indeed why?) the forming of the dolphins starts on the lathe. For the dolphins to perform their 'supporting role' convincingly it is important that their undersides fit snugly against the stem and base of the tazza, and their tails touch the underside of the shell dish. The lathe enables us to create exactly the same profile on both surfaces. It also helps get the external profile of all three dolphins the same by setting the position of their mouth, forehead, dorsal fin and tail into the lime block before they are separated. Finally, the lathe provides a quick and efficient method of undercutting the tail – rotation allows wood to be shaved away quickly and thinly without the pressures and shocks involved in hand carving. Although the lathe work in preparing the dolphins looks a little fiddly, it greatly simplifies the carving stage of the project.

SCALE DRAWING OF THE DOLPHIN TAZZA ON A 1IN (25MM) GRID. ENLARGE THE DRAWING TO THE REQUIRED SIZE.

TURNING THE DOLPHIN BLOCK

1 First, make a full-size drawing of the tazza, with the dolphins in profile, and several 'cylinders' of wood. To make the underside of the dolphins fit the tazza, create a 'cardboard cut-out' of the inside profile of the dolphins (the curve of the stem, base and dish) and cut it in half at its narrowest point. This will allow you to hollow out the centre of the block of lime from each end, effectively creating a 'negative' of the stem of the tazza.

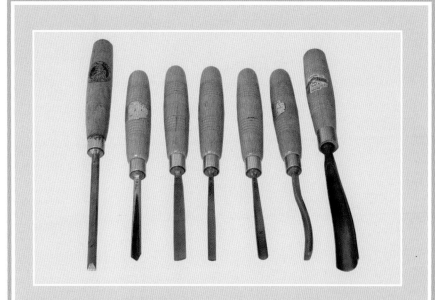

TOOLS AND MATERIALS

Wood: 'Dolphins' formed from a block of lime (*tilia* spp), 8in diameter x 6^1/$_2$in high (203 x 165mm) 'Tazza' sections in sapele (*entandrophragma cylindricum*): base 8in diameter x 2^1/$_2$in thick (203 x 64mm), stem 3^3/$_4$in diameter x 5^1/$_2$in high (95 x 140mm), dish 10in diameter x 3^1/$_2$in thick (254 x 89mm), feet 3@ 2^1/$_2$in long x 1^1/$_4$in wide x 1in high (64 x 32 x 25mm)

Adhesive: PVA Wood Adhesive

Tools: Woodturning lathe (see page 13) and appropriate turning tools (not illustrated). *From left to right:* ^{1}/$_4$in (6mm) fine-ground flat chisel, V-tool, ^{3}/$_8$in (10mm) No. 3 gouge, ^{1}/$_4$in (6mm) No. 5 gouge, ^{5}/$_16$in (8mm) No. 8 gouge, ^{5}/$_16$in (8mm) No. 8 curved gouge, ^{5}/$_8$in (16mm) No. 9 curved gouge

Finishing materials: French polish, acrylic gesso (with yellow food colour added), water-based gilding size, 23^3/$_4$-carat double gold leaf (about 25 leaves)

2 For the dolphin section, you need a block of lime 8in diameter x 6^1/$_2$in high (203 x 165mm). Mount it between centres on the lathe, put a spigot in the 'tail' end to fit your chuck, and square off the ends. Turn the main diameters of the external profile of the dolphins at this stage, measuring off the drawing with callipers.

3 Remove the tailstock and, with the upper 'tail' end held in the chuck, hollow the inner profile of the lower 'head' end. It is easier if you first use a 1¼in (32mm) Forstner bit to drill through the centre of the block.

4 As you hollow what will be the part of the dolphin that sits against the base and lower half of the stem, keep checking with the bottom half of the cardboard cut-out until it fits exactly.

5 Now remount the block by the opposite end. Because the end has been hollowed, make up a flat plywood disc 8in (203mm) in diameter, screw a faceplate to it and screw it to the lime block, using the tailstock to centre it.

6 Hollow out the tail end to fit the other half of the cardboard cut-out. Finish off the outer profile of the dolphins, and undercut the tail overhang so it is about ⅛in (3mm) thick at the outer edge.

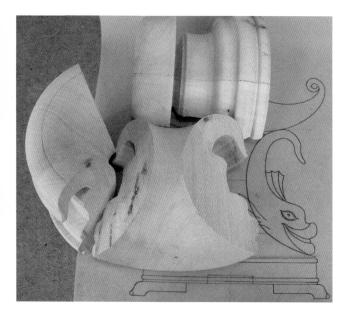

TURNING THE TAZZA

7 Remove the plywood plate and cut the block into three equal segments of 120 degrees. As they come apart the profile of the dolphins appears.

8 The tazza needs to be turned before carving the dolphins so the stem can be adjusted to give an exact fit to the inside of the dolphin block by 'offering up' the dolphin segments during turning. Prepare a 3³/₄in diameter x 5¹/₂in high (95 x 140mm) cylinder for the stem, and an 8in diameter x 2¹/₂in thick (203 x 64mm) blank for the base. Turn a spigot in the stem and a mortise to match in the base. Glue the stem to the base using the tailstock to centre and compress the joint while it sets.

9 Shape the base and stem to fit the inside of the dolphin blocks. Measure the diameters off the drawing first, then test-fit the lime. Put a 2in (50mm) mortise in the top of the stem.

10 Mount the 10in diameter x 3¹/₂in thick (254 x 89mm) bowl blank on a faceplate. Turn a 2in (50mm) spigot on the underside to fit the mortise in the stem. Start turning the underside of the bowl.

11 Continually test the fit of the stem and the dolphin blocks until the dolphin tail fits snugly against the underside of the bowl.

12 Remount the bowl by the spigot, and turn the inside so the bowl wall is about $^3/\sin$ (10mm) thick. Make a $^7/\sin$ (22mm) rounded rim around the edge (this will form the scroll at the back of the shell).

CARVING THE SHELL DISH

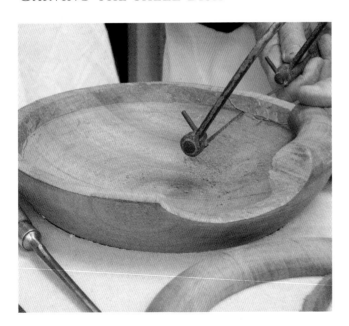

13 The turned bowl gives us the basis of the dish – which now has to be carved into a something resembling a scallop shell. Mark out the section of the bowl rim that will be the scroll. Cut away the rest of the rim at its thickest point (you can use a jigsaw) and blend it in with the inside of the bowl. Cut out the two 'scalloped' sections beside the scroll with a coping saw.

14 Carefully mark out and carve the concave shell markings in the inside of the bowl, making them as regular and natural-looking as possible. (See 'Work Holding' Tip on page 171.)

15 Do the same with the convex markings on the underside. Align the concave and convex sections on the inside and outside so they form a series of curved undulations at the edge about $^1/\!sin$ (3mm) thick.

16 Carve the 'hinge' part of the rim into a classical scroll, blending the scalloped sections into it. Slope the outer edges of the shell to accentuate the concave/convex undulations.

MAKING THE FEET

17 The three feet of the tazza are based on a smaller version of the scallop shell. First rough out the feet with a bandsaw or coping saw – each foot must be the same thickness so the tazza stands level. Shape the shell with a $^3/\!sin$ (10mm) No. 3 gouge, then use a V-tool and an inverted No. 5 gouge to carve the ribs of the shell.

> **TIP:** MAKING PARTS FIT
> When several pieces have to fit exactly together, make an accurate full-size drawing and measure-off from the drawing at each stage as you work. Trace cardboard templates where appropriate and use them as profiles. Use callipers for diameters. With care, it should all fit together at the end.

ASSEMBLING THE TAZZA

18 Glue the shell dish onto the stem, with the grain direction at right-angles to the base for the best appearance. Screw and glue the feet in place at 120° intervals directly under where the dolphin heads will be. Give the tazza about four coats of French polish.

CARVING THE DOLPHINS

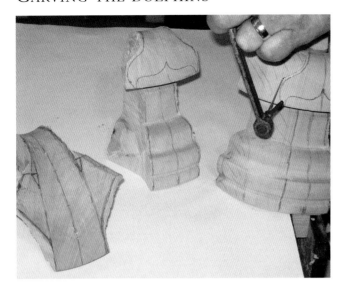

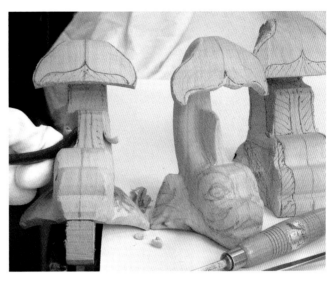

19 To carve the dolphins out of the three blocks made on the lathe, start by cutting off the spare wood at the sides. Mark a centreline on each of the dolphin blocks, and draw on the side profiles so the width of the body is roughly equal to the thickness. Take care to leave the side fins at full width, and the end of the tail about 3½in (63mm) wide. Rough out the profiles with a coping saw. To get them all looking identical it is best to complete one stage on all three dolphins before moving on to the next stage.

20 Shape the sides of the body into the side fins, dorsal fin and tail. Measure with callipers to get each dolphin exactly the same width at each point. The moulded curve of the underside (including the side fins) must be left so the body sits naturally against the curve of the tazza. At this stage we start to reap the benefits of the work done on the lathe.

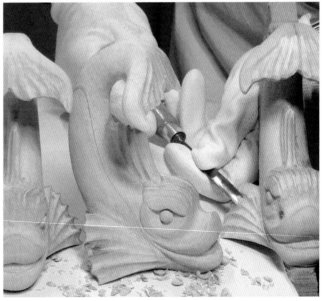

21 Carve the detail of the face, mouth and eyes. Make sure both eyes are in the same position so everything looks straight from the front, top and sides.

22 Use a No. 8 gouge to carve the detail on the fins and tail, giving them traditional 'fishy' features.

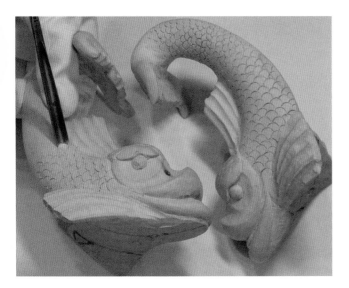

GILDING AND FINISHING

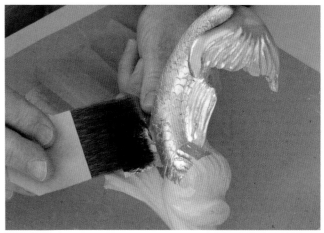

23 Finally, carve simple scales all over the body from behind the head to the curve of the tail by 'pricking' with a No. 8 gouge. Keep the scales in proportion to the width of the body, getting slightly smaller towards the tail.

24 Seal the finished dolphins with sander-sealer. Apply several coats of acrylic gesso (only one over the scales but about six everywhere else) with a little yellow food colouring added, over the course of a day. Next day, apply a coat of gilding size and, when touch-dry, apply the gold leaf. To get a true eighteenth-century finish the dolphins are gilded with real gold leaf ($23^3/_4$-carat). If you use imitation gold leaf you will need to seal it against tarnishing. Genuine gold leaf needs no sealer, but may wear if handled frequently.

25 Finally, complete the assembly by gluing the dolphins carefully in position with a quick-setting glue. Mark the position for the dolphins on the tazza and scrape off a thin strip of the French polish to give a good glue bond. Carefully glue the dolphins in place without getting glue on the French polish. What started off as several pieces of wood whizzing round on a lathe at last becomes an elegant table decoration fit, perhaps not for a King, but maybe for a Dauphin.

TIP: WORK HOLDING

To hold the bowl while carving the shell detail (photos 13 and 14), cut a 6in (152mm) circle in a piece of board and sit the bowl in it. Keep the bowl in the chuck but remove the chuck from the lathe and grip it in a vice between two softwood 'cushions'. To carve the underside of the shell dish (photo 15), make a wooden disc to fit the inside of the dish and fix it to a 1in (25mm) board, overhanging the edge so the scroll sits clear. Clamp the board to the bench and place the dish upside down over the disc. To hold the dolphins, cut a piece of wood to the profile of the dolphin's underside and screw through into the dolphin block, taking care not to damage the visible surface. Hold this block in the vice (photos 19, 20 and 22).

Louis XV Style

Project 19
LARGE-SCALE ARABESQUE

This is the only project in this book which is not scaled to fit the average room, but it is included for three reasons: you may have a room or hallway that would suit a large carving; you can scale it down to suit a smaller room if you wish; and the techniques involved in large-scale carving are useful to know and can often be applied to smaller carvings.

It was created for a family friend in America who wanted a large and striking carving for her spacious New England house. It is designed around arabesque elements – a style of ornament which, as the name suggests, derives from Arabian roots. Its key features are swirling and intertwining vines. It was popular as surface decoration in the Renaissance period, and enjoyed a revival (like most styles) in Victorian times.

Arabesque patterns are normally symmetrical but for artistic reasons I made this design asymmetrical, taking care to balance the various elements. To make it lighter and more sinuous I 'pierced' it extensively, in keeping with the Middle Eastern door screens that were its progenitors. A solid panel of this size would just look like a giant slab of wood.

When designing a large carving, just because it is bigger doesn't mean you should cram the extra space full of detail.

From a distance it will look 'busy' and the effect will be lost. It is a good idea to draw your design about quarter-size to get a better feel for the amount of detail you should include.

Size also impacts on the design in a way that may not be immediately obvious – the weight. In this arabesque design some of the smaller 'vines' are not there just to look pretty – they have an essential role in supporting the physical structure. Without them, several parts of the main 'branch' would be under great strain and could split along the grain.

If you decide to tackle this project full size, read it first so you know what you are taking on – it is not for the faint-hearted or weak-backed. It weighs 77 pounds (35kg) when first assembled, and requires a considerable investment in timber. But the instructions for scaling up the drawing allow you to make it any size you want, so just decide what suits you best and make it that size.

1837–1901 Victorian

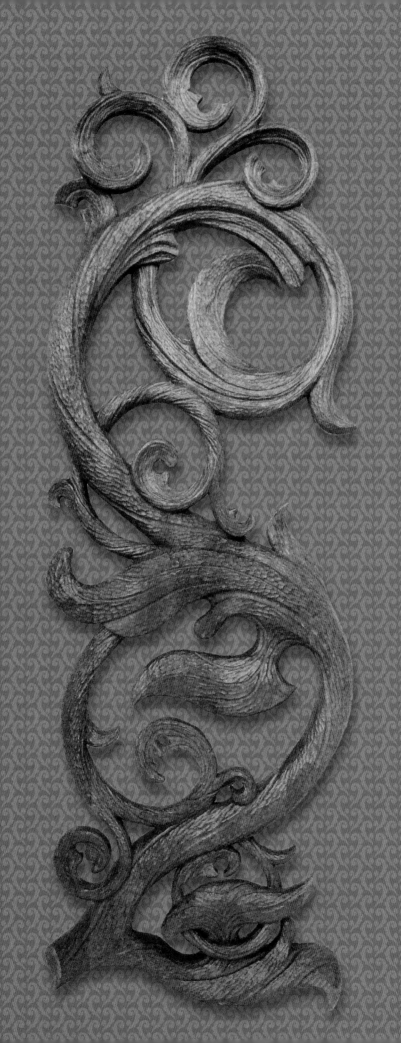

SCALE DRAWING OF THE ARABESQUE PIERCED PANEL ON A 1IN (25MM) GRID. ENLARGE THE DRAWING TO THE REQUIRED SIZE.

1837–1901 Victorian

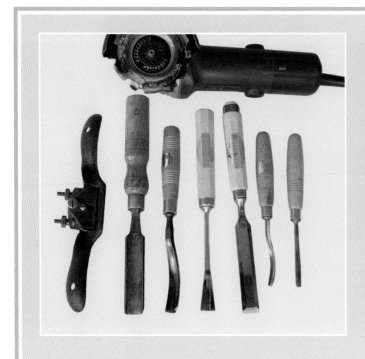

Tools and materials

Wood: Sapele mahogany (*entandrophragma cylindricum*): 33ft (10 metres) of planed '4in (100mm) nominal' square section (planed size $3^3/4$in /95mm square section). To get the 22in (560mm) width requires six lengths of timber, each piece averaging about 66in (1.68 metres). Approximate weight: before cutting: 116 pounds (53kg); before carving: 77 pounds (35kg), finished weight 43 pounds (20kg)

Adhesive: PVA Wood Adhesive

Tools: Bandsaw (see page 13) (*from top and left to right*) Arbortech rotary carver, spokeshave, 1in (25mm) No. 6 gouge, $^5/8$in (16mm) No. 9 curved gouge, $^3/4$in (20mm) No. 3 fishtail gouge, $^3/4$in (20mm) flat chisel, $^5/16$in (8mm) No. 8 curved gouge, $^5/16$in (8mm) No. 8 gouge

Finishing material: French polish

Timber and lamination

1 For this carving you need to create a large sapele panel 66in high x 22in wide x 4in thick (1670 x 560 x 100mm). Because of its size, it will need laminating and, so the joins don't show, it is important to choose pieces of timber that, as far as possible, are straight grained and all the same colour. They must be milled to a uniform width, with straight clean edges, and fully seasoned to avoid warping. Because the design is for a pierced carving it makes sense to remove unwanted wood before joining the strips. Hacking out voids in a 4in (100mm) thick hardwood panel would be slow and laborious.

Scaling up

2 The 1in (25mm) grid on the quarter-size drawing is scaled up to full size by marking out a large board or sheet of paper with 4in (100mm) squares. Give each square a grid-reference and simply copy whatever lines you see in that square from the small sheet to the large sheet. Tidy up the lines afterwards and you will have a full-size version of your small drawing. You can scale a drawing up or down to any size you want using this method by adjusting the size of the squares.

MARKING OUT AND CUTTING

3 Before cutting, the full-size design must be traced onto tracing paper and marked out in vertical strips exactly the same width as the timbers ($3^3/4$in/ 95mm). The strips will contain some odd shapes, many of which will need temporary support struts left in to avoid snapping thin sections. The joins will need compressing with several large F-clamps while the glue sets, and it is difficult to get a clamp to hold on a curve. Working out a clamping and gluing sequence is essential before cutting, so you can leave square-edged 'flanges' to clamp against where required. You must ensure the clamp pressure acts directly on the join and not on an unsupported section.

4 Trace each strip of the pattern onto each piece of sapele using carbon paper, together with the grid-square identifying letters so everything can be pieced together later.

GLUING UP

5 Cut out each piece on the bandsaw.

6 Exploded view – the giant jigsaw puzzle of 29 pieces ready for assembly. Mark the grid lines and square references onto the wood to aid identification and lining up of individual pieces. The temporary supports and clamping flanges (marked here in green) can be cut out after gluing.

STARTING TO CARVE

7 Because of the complexity of the pattern, gluing and clamping needs to be done a few pieces at a time over several days. Both faces of each join must have a complete covering of adhesive. Starting from the middle and working outwards, assemble sections and clamp them firmly together with F-clamps tightly enough to give an invisible join. Use greaseproof paper when gluing to stop the timbers sticking to the surface they are laying on. Leave them clamped at least twelve hours before removing the clamps and adding more pieces. After about three days you will have the structure for the arabesque panel, and be ready to start carving.

8 A bigger carving needs bigger tools. I mainly used gouges ranging from ⁵/sin (16mm) up to 1in (25mm). Large tools have a wider cutting edge, so the resistance to pushing is proportionally greater and you spend a lot of time whacking away with a mallet. Carving starts by marking the overlaps of the different vines, branches and leaves. They need to flow over, under and around one another in a way that looks natural and gives the panel some 'depth'. The 4in (100mm) thick timbers are needed for this carving as they have the same 'visual depth' as a 1in (25mm) thickness on a panel a quarter the size.

9 The next step is to 'establish the levels' of the various elements. Although I normally prefer to carve with hand tools, with such a large amount of hard timber to remove an Arbortech rotary carver speeds up the job. Grind out the bulk of the wood down to just above the required level.

10 A spokeshave helps to shape the curved sections. This is physically hard work, but better than hammering away with a mallet for hours on end. Chisels and gouges are needed for the tight corners and overlaps that other tools can't reach.

Arabesque

TAKING A STEP BACK

UNDERCUTTING

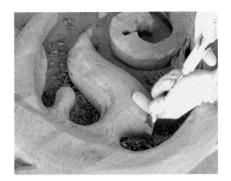

11 When working on a large carving laying on its back, your focus tends to be on the part of the carving you are working on. So you don't lose the 'bigger picture' you need to stand it up frequently and take a step (or several steps) back. Look at it from all the angles it will be seen to make sure you are getting the effect you want before moving on to the 'undercutting' stage.

12 The purpose of undercutting is to make the leaves look thinner and the stems and branches look naturally round. On a solid carving undercutting can seem a bit daunting, but on a pierced carving it is simply a case of turning it face down and attacking it from the back. I say 'attacking' because much of it is just removing bulk. The Arbortech is by far the best tool for this job.

13 There are some tricks to under-cutting that apply whether a carving is large or small. If it is going to be seen mainly from the front, you need to give the 'leaves' thin edges but leave an increasing thickness behind them as you move away from the edge. That way you can retain enough strength in the wood to avoid pieces snapping off during or after carving. Thin down the edges of the 'leaves' with chisels and gouges.

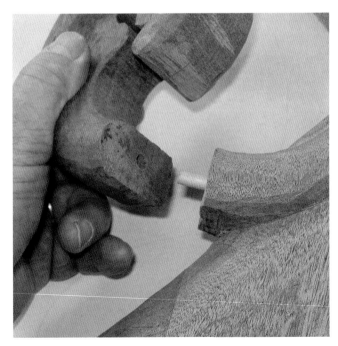

14 Finish the sides of the branches and stems with spokeshaves.

15 Strength is especially important where a thin section extends across the grain. Wood has much greater strength along the grain, but can easily fracture if supported only by a thin, cross-grained section. Despite my efforts to design-out weak joints, I found one while undercutting and had to re-fix it using a dowel to give extra cross-grain support.

SURFACE DECORATION

16 An arabesque should lead the eye around the pattern in a whirl of 'movement'. Natural vines not only curl around one another but also spiral along their own length. Along each vine and branch carve a series of grooves rotating gradually in a spiral, using larger and smaller gouges in proportion to the thickness. In between these spiral lines, texture the surface by making little scoops with the same gouges to give the appearance of bark, keeping the same directional flow and the same differential in size.

FINISHING

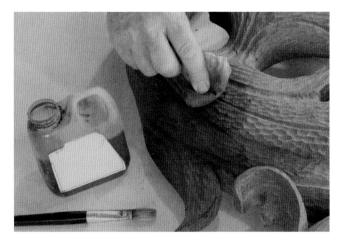

17 French polish is not always recommended for carvings, as the shiny finish accentuates every irregularity in the surface, but with a bark texture like this, accentuating the irregularities has a positive effect. Apply the first coat of French polish with a brush, then rub it in with a cloth, followed by two more coats applied by cloth. This finish brings out the dark rich colour of the sapele, and provides just the right amount of reflection to give it a lively sparkle.

18 The finished carving weighs about 43 pounds (20kg). Some of the individual laminations may be visible at first in some lights, but will usually darken to the same shade before long.

19 The decorative effect of a carving of this scale is quite stunning in a room or hallway that is big enough to take it. Here it has been mounted 4in (100mm) away from the wall using long screw-in bolts with covering sleeves. Atmospheric lighting brings out the warmth of the sapele and French polish.

Arabesque

Project 20

GRINLING GIBBONS FOLIAGE

This project is based on a small section of a real Grinling Gibbons limewood chimneypiece at Belton House, Grantham, Lincolnshire. I have taken the lowest portion of a long festoon and adapted the design to make it easier to carve and suitable for display in an ordinary home.

Grinling Gibbons (1648–1721) was one of the greatest carvers of all time. He lifted decorative carving to a standard never seen before and rarely seen since his passing. The limewood foliage carvings Gibbons created were so light, so naturalistic and so visually stunning that he became the master carver of choice for the palaces of England during his lifetime. Visit any of the places he worked on and you will be amazed by the swags and festoons of flowers, fruit, fowl and game that were his trademark. Gibbons' style of foliage carving was probably influenced by the Dutch still-life painters of seventeenth-century Rotterdam where he grew up and served his apprenticeship (he was 19 when his parents took him back to their native England). A Gibbons carving is a still-life in wood – there is nothing stylized about it – it is as near to nature as you can get using wood as your medium.

The method of construction is the key to tackling a Gibbons' carving. He built up his carvings in layers, with many attachments carved separately. However, with the aid of modern adhesives, we can carve in smaller sections and assemble them more easily than Gibbons could have done. To carvers used to working on a single block of wood, this assembly process can seem like a cross between flower arranging and making model aeroplanes, but it works and it makes the job much easier.

The term 'easier' is relative when dealing with a Gibbons carving as it is still a very complex piece. But, once you build up a little confidence with the three-dimensional nature of working 'in the round', the depth of excavation, the volume of undercutting, and the patient paring away required to create leaves and petals with ultra-thin edges, you will find you can produce stems, leaves and flowers that get very close to the look of a Gibbons foliage carving.

SCALE DRAWING OF THE GRINLING GIBBONS FOLIAGE PATTERN ON A 1IN (25MM) GRID. ENLARGE THE DRAWING TO THE REQUIRED SIZE.

1603–1714 Jacobean and Stuart

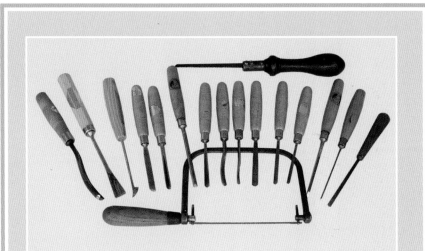

Tools and Materials

Wood: Lime (*tilia* spp). The base section must be at least 19in long x 5in wide x 2^1/$_2$in thick (483 x 127 x 64mm). There are many permutations for the middle and front sections of the carving, but they are best cut from two more pieces the same size as the base section by careful arrangement of the tracings.

Tools (*from left to right*): padsaw, coping saw, ^{5}/$_8$in (16mm) No. 9 curved gouge, ^{3}/$_4$in (20mm) No. 3 fishtail gouge, ^{5}/$_8$in (16mm)

hooked skew chisel, ^{3}/$_8$in (10mm) skew chisel, V-tool, ^{1}/$_4$in (6mm) fine-ground flat chisel, ^{5}/$_{16}$in (8mm) No. 8 gouge, ^{5}/$_{16}$in (8mm) No. 8 curved gouge, ^{3}/$_{16}$in (5mm) bent chisel, ^{3}/$_8$in (10mm) No. 3 gouge, ^{1}/$_4$in (6mm) No. 5 gouge, ^{3}/$_{16}$in (5mm) No. 5 gouge, ^{1}/$_8$in (3mm) chisel, ^{1}/$_{16}$in (2mm) chisel, ^{1}/$_4$in (6mm) No. 5 round-end gouge

Adhesive: PVA Wood Adhesive
Abrasives: 120 and 240 grit
Finishes: None

Carving the Base Section

1 The base section (part 1 on the drawing) forms the 'undergrowth' that the more 'high-flying' parts of the carving are anchored to. The process starts conventionally enough by tracing the pattern onto a block of lime 19 x 5 x 2^1/$_2$in (483 x 127 x 64mm) and cutting around the outside with the bandsaw. But, unlike a normal relief carving, this one will be finished almost 'in the round' so the outline pattern is only a guide. As you carve individual elements you will need to make adjustments to get a good three-dimensional form.

2 Rough out the levels of the various elements at the lower end of the carving. Each will be carved in the round, so leave enough room. The position of the chrysanthemum-like flower with its back to us is critical as the stems of the foremost crocus flowers pass over its stem and under one of its petals. Scoop out large hollows each side where the pear and rose will be placed later.

> **TIP:** BARE WOOD FINISH
> When a carving is to have a bare wood finish, make sure you keep it clean. Wear carving gloves, and only use wax colouring pencils when drawing on the wood, as graphite creates a black dust that gets ground in.

3 Modelling the flowers and fruit is a slow and tricky process, as each piece must be rounded, hollowed and partially undercut so it appears detached from its neighbours, yet part of a group. The degree of separation in a Gibbons' carving is much greater than in a normal relief carving, so a lot of excavating is needed to create the spaces between the objects and their stems. The crocus flowers can be hollowed firstly with a drill, then a No. 8 gouge. All leaves and petals must be pared to an edge that is virtually sharp. Everything must be modelled as close to nature as possible. You can do some undercutting from the front, then turn it over to get at the underside.

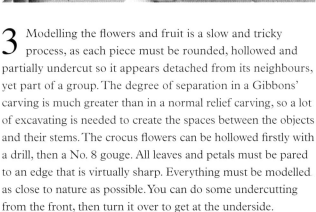

4 Pare away the underside gently with sharp tools to avoid breaking off thin pieces. Smaller tools exert less pressure than large tools, so use them on the thinner sections. Leave thicker sections for structural support where they do not show, but try to get it so that from the front and sides all the elements appear to be nearly as thin as they would be in nature. ***This process of roughing out levels, modelling the front, and undercutting from behind is repeated throughout this carving.***

5 Moving to the top end, create a supporting structure of interlaced stems throughout the carving. Remember that the base section will have to support the whole carving when it is hanging on the wall, and thin sections should be 'braced' against another stem or flower to reduce the risk of breakages. As you carve down, create new surface layers for carving flowers among the undergrowth – they add depth and naturalism.

6 The central 'flower stack' is the structure to which the outer sprays of flowers and stems will be fixed. It is largely hidden by later additions so it is carved as background foliage. Use a padsaw or coping saw to separate the 'petals' into at least three layers vertically (when on its back) and shape them so they curve in opposite directions at each level. Give the petals sharp edges.

7 Finish the area where the rose and pear will be fixed by separating the various stems and carving some flowers that will show around the edge of the pear. Carve the outer rose petals that will be on the base section on the right-hand side of the rose (the rose will be added separately). After undercutting from behind, the base section is now finished.

LEFT PROFILE

FRONT VIEW

RIGHT PROFILE

ADDING THE MIDDLE LAYER

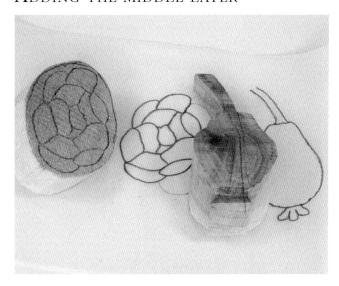

8 Trace the pear and the rose (parts 2a and 2b on the drawing) onto some lime 2¹/₂in (64mm) thick, and rough out the shape on the bandsaw. I have used some darker lime with figuring for the pear, but this is optional.

9 Carve the pear in the round to the size and shape of a real pear, including a stem and a 'blossom end'. Mould it to fit the base section and glue it in place. Carve the rose to fit the outer petals already on the base (it is easier to work if you glue it in place to finish it off). A ⁵/₈in (16mm) hooked skew chisel is a good tool for carving the tight angles where the rose petals overlap.

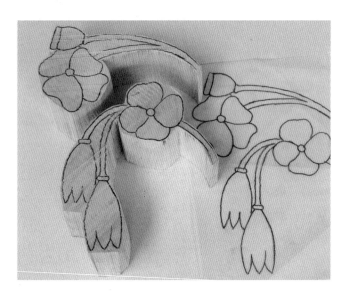

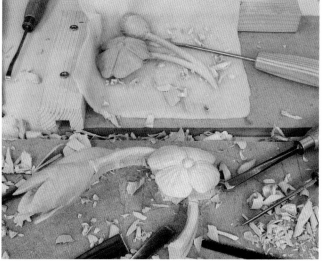

10 Continuing with the middle level of add-ons, trace the two left-hand sections of flowers and their stems (parts 3a and 3b on the drawing) onto a block of wood about 2in (51mm) thick and cut around them with the band saw. When carving thin stems, align the wood so the grain runs along the stem if you can. Thin cross-grain sections are inherently weak.

11 Work-holding can be a problem with these fragile detached pieces. Start with the piece screwed to a backing board from the underneath (foreground). When you have shaped the detail and partially undercut from the front, detach it from the board and finish it off on a board with raised corners. Push your gouges towards the corners and away from your fingers. Undercut by turning the piece upside down on a cushion of non-slip matting and pare away carefully. ***This process is repeated for all the remaining pieces.***

12 Continue the add-ons with this large and rather floppy-looking flower (part 4 on the drawing). Cut it from wood about $1^1/2$in (38mm) thick, with the grain running along the two longest petals, and carve it to this odd but very natural-looking contorted shape, sloping down at the ends and edges so it has a slightly 'domed' overall shape. Undercut it to a sharp edge all round, but leave enough thickness hidden underneath to prevent it breaking across the grain.

13 Assemble the left and right flower sections onto the base. Using the framework of stems, the large central flower, the poppy head (left) and the 'pansy' flower (right) as supports, glue the flowers in place with as many points of contact as you can find (at least three). Make sure you get the positioning right in relation to the whole carving, allowing for the next layer of add-ons.

ADDING THE FRONT LAYER

14 Start the front layer with this small group of crocus flowers (part 5 on the drawing), which will sit just below the centre of the carving. Rough out the three flower heads from a block 2in (51mm) thick using the bandsaw and coping saw before shaping with the usual gouges. As with all the crocus-type flowers, the centres can be drilled out before hollowing with gouges (do this before you carve the thin stems as the twisting of the drill can snap them). The 'daisy' flower at the top end not only forms part of the 'undergrowth' but also provides a broad base for gluing to the central flower stack.

Limewood Baroque

16a

16b

15 The left-hand flower spray (part 6 on the drawing), also carved from a 2in (51mm) thickness, has four crocus flowers and three quite flat pea pods. The flower at the top again provides a gluing point and also strengthens the curve in the stem where it turns across the grain.

16 The right-hand spray consists of a whole bunch of smaller crocus flowers coming off an upper and lower group of stems. This is best carved in two pieces (parts 7a and 7b on the drawing), each from 2in (51mm) thickness. Photo 16a shows the longer rear section, and photo 16b shows the slightly shorter forward section. Each has a flower at the stem end for fixing to the central flower stack. The rear spray also has another flower at the bottom end to provide a support fixing to the pear.

17 These flower sprays are glued to the central flower stack by their fixing flowers, layered over one another. Now we just need to cover up the joins. On Gibbons' original carving the central point was finished just with a cluster of the small 'daisy' flowers. That was fine as part of a much larger carving, but for ours to stand alone as a complete piece it needs something more substantial to finish off the centre.

1603–1714 Jacobean and Stuart

THE FINISHING TOUCH

LEFT VIEW   BACK VIEW   RIGHT VIEW

18 To give us our centre piece I have repeated the rose which appears at the bottom of the carving, with some adjustment for its 'centre stage' position (part 8 on the drawing). Rough this out from a block 3 x 4 x 2in (76 x 101 x 51mm) and shape the petals in layers, in the same manner as previously.

20 The carving is now finished. The photographs above give a clear illustration of structure. Despite its overall size of 19 x 10 x 5in (483 x 254 x 127mm) it weighs only 1$\frac{3}{4}$ pounds (0.8 kg), as it is mostly fresh air. The lime is best left untreated and will darken gradually to a light brown (some bits more than others, if your wood is not all from the same tree).

19 Glue the rose in place so it nestles snugly among the flowers and stems in the centre of the carving, facing slightly upwards. You may have to reshape some of the 'undergrowth' to get it to sit properly.

21 Mount the carving on the wall in a well-lit place where it is seen face-on. It is quite fragile compared to more solid carvings, so make sure your chosen location is somewhere it will not get damaged. Oh... and I suggest you take care of the dusting personally, by blowing the dust away!

ABOUT THE AUTHOR

Steve Bisco has been carving as a hobby for 25 years. He is a regular contributor to *Woodcarving* magazine, specializing in decorative carving in period styles. He is inspired by a love of historic buildings and aims to capture the spirit of a period in pieces for display in the 'home gallery'. Having visited most of the stately homes and palaces of Britain, as well as many in Europe and New England, his mission is to make period decorative carving accessible to the average hobby woodcarver in the average house.

Steve grew up on an island near the ancient Roman town of Colchester, England, where he still lives with his wife Jenny. They have a daughter Josephine who lives near New York, and a son Toby who lives in London.

BIBLIOGRAPHY, LOCATIONS AND WEBSITE LINKS

Project 4 ARTS AND CRAFTS FLOWER PANEL: Blackwell – The Arts & Crafts House, Bowness on Windermere, Cumbria, England (*www.blackwell.org.uk*)

Project 5 'HOLKER' OLIVE PANEL: Holker Hall, Cark-in-Cartmel, Cumbria, England (*www.holker.co.uk*)

Project 7 GOTHIC WINDOW: Pugin, A.C.
Pugin's Gothic Ornament (first published 1828)
Dover Publications (1987)
(*www.doverpublications.com*)
ISBN 0-486-25500-X

Project 8 THE PEACOCK OF RIGA: Riga, Latvia – Art Nouveau (*www. rigalatvia.net/en_art_nouveau.html*)

Project 9 THE DRAGON OF EYE: Colling, James K.
Victorian Foliage Designs (first published 1865)
Dover Publications (2003)
(*www.doverpublications.com*)
ISBN 0-486-42742-0

Project 11 PUGIN COLUMN TABLE: Hill, Rosemary *God's Architect – Pugin & the Building of Romantic Britain*
Penguin/Allen Lane (2007)
(*www.penguin.com*)
ISBN 978-0-713-99499-5

St Giles Church, Cheadle, Staffordshire, England (*www.bbc.co.uk/stoke/360/stgiles*)

Project 12 FRUIT-AND-FLOWER FESTOON: Alnwick Castle, Northumberland, England (*www.alnwickcastle.com*)

Sudbury Hall, Derbyshire, England (*www.nationaltrust.org.uk/sudburyhall*)

Project 15 CHIPPENDALE RIBBON FESTOON:
Chippendale, Thomas
The Gentleman & Cabinet Maker's Director (1762 edition)
Dover Publications (1966)
(*www.doverpublications.com*)
ISBN 0-486-21601-2

Project 16 ROCOCO MIRROR FRAME: Peterhof Grand Palace, St Petersburg, Russia (*www.saint-petersburg.com/peterhof*)

Project 20 GRINLING GIBBONS FOLIAGE:
Belton House, Grantham, Lincolnshire, England (*www.nationaltrust.org.uk/belton*)

Esterly, David
Grinling Gibbons and the Art of Carving
V&A Publications (1998)
(*www.vandashop.com*)
ISBN 1-85177-256-1

INDEX

Names of projects are printed in **bold**.

To request a full catalogue of GMC titles, please contact:

GMC Publications Ltd

Castle Place, 166 High Street, Lewes, East Sussex, BN7 1XU, United Kingdom
Tel: +44 (0)1273 488005   Fax: +44 (0)1273 402866   www.thegmcgroup.com

Orders by credit card are accepted